Wholesome Worship

CHARLES GUSMER

FOREWORD BY
Balthasar Fischer

THE PASTORAL PRESS
WASHINGTON, DC

Acknowledgments

Acknowledgment is gratefully made to the publishers and others for granting permission to use again, sometimes in edited form, the following: "Liturgical Prayer," *Looking at Our Faith Series* (New York: William H. Sadlier Inc., 1985), pp. 1–7; "Making Worship Work," *Sign* 59:3 (November 1979), pp. 16–21; "Liturgy and Social Consciousness," (original title: "Parish Worship: Don't Forget Our Basics") *Church* 59:3 (Winter 1985), pp. 37–39; "Liturgy and Catechesis," unpublished address delivered at the 23rd Southwest Liturgical Conference Study Week (23 January, 1985); "A Bill of Rights: Liturgical Adaptation in America," *Worship* 51:4 (July 1977), pp. 283–289; "Celebrating Sunday Liturgy: Present and Future," *The Living Light* 14:1 (Spring 1977) pp. 94–102; "Is It Worship? Evaluating the Sunday Liturgy," *Living Worship* 14:10 (December 1978); "Is the Mass a Meal?" *Catholic Update* (Cincinnati: St. Anthony Messenger Press, 1977); "Toward a Spirituality of Daily Mass," *New Catholic World* 224:1342, pp. 182–185; "The Key to the Sacrament of Reconciliation," *New Catholic World* 227:1357, pp. 37–41; "General Sacramental Absolution and the Symbolic Language of Penance," *General Absolution: Toward a Deeper Understanding* (Chicago: Federation of Diocesan Liturgical Commissions, 1978), pp. 15–18; "Penance and Anointing of the Sick," *Reconciliation: The Continuing Agenda*, ed. by Robert J. Kennedy (Collegeville: The Liturgical Press, 1987), pp. 205–218; "Healing: Charism and Sacrament," *Church* 2:2 (Summer 1986), pp. 16–22; "Lent: Community Conversion," *Christian Initiation Resources* (New York: William H. Sadlier Inc., 1981) pp. 235–240; "Celebrating the Easter Season," *Christian Initiation Resources* (New York: William H. Sadlier Inc., 1982); "Ordinary Time: The Season of the Year," *Word on Worship* (Newsletter of the Worship Office, Archdiocese of Newark, N.J.) 1:4 (May/June 1982). Scriptural selections are taken from the *New American Bible*, Copyright © 1970 by the Confraternity of Christian Doctrine, Washington, D.C. All rights reserved. Excerpts from the English translation of the *Roman Calendar* c 1970, International Committee on English in the Liturgy, Inc. (ICEL); the English translation of the *Roman Missal* © 1973, ICEL; the English translation of the *Rite of Penance* © 1974, ICEL; the English translation of the *Rite of Anointing and Pastoral Care of the Sick* © 1974, ICEL; from the English translation of the *Rite of Christian Initiation of Adults* © 1985, ICEL. All rights reserved. Excerpts from the English translation of the Constitution on the Sacred Liturgy are from Walter M. Abbott, S.J., ed., *The Documents of Vatican II*, © 1966, America Press. All rights reserved.

The Pastoral Press
225 Sheridan Street, N.W.
Washington, D.C. 20011
(202) 723–1254

The Pastoral Press is the publications division of the National Association of Pastoral Musicians, a membership organization of musicians and clergy dedicated to fostering the art of musical liturgy.

To John and Carolyn,

Bill and Hope,

and my nieces and nephews

Foreword

Father Charles Gusmer, one of America's leading Roman Catholic liturgists today, earned his doctorate in 1970 at Trier, Germany under my guidance with a remarkable thesis on *The Ministry of Healing in the Church of England: An Ecumenical—Liturgical Study* (Alcuin Club, 1974). He had the good idea to mark the twenty-fifth anniversary of the Constitution on the Sacred Liturgy (4 December, 1988) and his own fiftieth birthday (11 October, 1988) by the publication of this selection of essays. They were all written in the aftermath of this unique event, the promulgation of the first document on the liturgy of the church ever produced by an ecumenical council.

With the high competence for which he is known among colleagues and students, he advances the goal he himself describes in chapter 2: after the end of the reform measures we have to claim the new house of post-conciliar liturgical rites as our home. The warmth of the word "home" pervades everything the author says or suggests about the liturgical life of the postconciliar church. He understands how to make this new home attractive and loveable to his readers, not merely by describing the changes but by opening the eyes of his readers to the theological rethinking which has been at work in these changes. With his insights from a *relecture* of sacramental theology, he combines a fine pastoral sense which avoids exaggerations, notes deviations, and points the way for further pastoral developments in this rapidly changing world of ours. In all the various questions treated, he betrays a rare combination of scholarly thoroughness and pastoral common sense.

There is one center which all the articles published here encircle: Christ's saving mystery, which has gained such an unheard of impact in North America by the swift and competent implementation of the Rite of Christian Initiation of Adults. This mystery, reactualized among us in the liturgy, should once again—and this is the objective of each and every page of this book—be "the summit towards which the activity of the Church is directed and at the same time the fountain from which all her power flows" (Constitution on the Liturgy, no. 10).

Balthasar Fischer

Contents

Introduction

The life of the author of these articles is inseparably bound up with the Second Vatican Council. My first day of theological studies at Innsbruck coincided with the day Pope John XXIII convened a council which was to alter profoundly the course of the church. After priesthood ordination in 1966 and subsequent doctoral studies in liturgy under Balthasar Fischer at Trier, I was able to assist in the implementation of the liturgical renewal emanating from the pontificate of the great Paul VI. I am grateful to the respective archbishops of Newark—Thomas A. Boland, Peter Leo Gerety, and Theodore E. McCarrick—for the privilege to instruct and form a whole generation of priests in the knowledge and love of the sacred liturgy at Immaculate Conception Seminary, first at Darlington, now an integral part of Seton Hall University.

These articles in a sense follow the course of those twenty years. For this collection, however, the bibliographical references have been fully updated and the text partially revised. The references to the catechumenate, for example, correspond to the revised Rite of Christian Initiation of Adults.

If any personal deepening has occurred, it would be a more existential appropriation of how the active participation in the liturgy is, in the words of Pius X, "the primary and indispensable source of the true Christian spirit." The public prayer of the church, especially the eucharist, makes present the mystery of Christ, which is the source of all Christian life and prayer. The mystery of Christ crucified and risen celebrated in worship

1

immerses us into the life of the Triune God, constitutes us as church, the Body of Christ, and represents the very healing and liberation for which the world yearns. The same paschal mystery, which enables us to participate in the priestly office of Jesus Christ, evokes from us a response of love expressed in an attitude of dedication and surrender to God and self-giving service of others. This is how Christians live out the mystery of Christ, the answer to the meaning of human existence, in which life always issues forth from death. We live in Christ; his triumphant and life-giving cross is our salvation and hope.

I am grateful to my family and friends for their love and support, my colleagues in the field of liturgy and at the seminary for their inspiration, and my students—seminarians and lay ministers—who helped stimulate these ideas. Special thanks are due to Larry Johnson of The Pastoral Press for his encouragement and guidance.

The universal Church of Christ, and therefore each particular Church, exists in order to pray. In prayer the human person expresses his or her nature; the community expresses its vocation; the Church reaches out to God. In prayer the Church attains fellowship with the Father and with his Son, Jesus Christ. In prayer the Church expresses her Trinitarian life because she directs herself to the Father, undergoes the action of the Holy Spirit, and lives fully her relationship with Christ. Indeed, she experiences herself as the Body of Christ, as the mystical Christ.

Address of John Paul II to the U.S. Bishops (10 June 1988)

Ritual
and
Its Many Dimensions

CHAPTER 1

Liturgical Prayer

In order to develop our topic of liturgical prayer, let us first ask: What is prayer altogether? Prayer is the response-ability to engage in a dialogue of communion with a God who is Father, Son, and Spirit. The mystery of the Trinity is not merely a doctrine of three persons in one God to which we profess belief. The Trinity is the mystery of the inner life of God in which we are invited to share. God the Father is the first person of the Trinity who communicates himself to us in a way that is like that of a mother giving life to a child. The Son, the second person of the Trinity, is our risen Lord and best friend, Jesus Christ: he is the human face of God and the mediator between God and the human race. The Holy Spirit is the third person of the Trinity who brings about in us this sharing in the life of the Trinity. Thus, to be a Christian means to be in relationship with the Trinity of Father, Son, and Spirit: three different ways we experience God. To pray means to enter into conscious dialogue with God Father, Son, and Spirit and to make transparent the dialogue of communion with the gracious divine presence which is going on all the time.

There are different dimensions to our life of prayer. At times we pray alone, conversing with God in the stillness of our hearts, for God calls us by our first name. At other times we pray together in the public worship of the church, for God always saves us as a people. This common prayer together

5

constitutes liturgical prayer. Liturgical prayer is what we do together in church as the community of the church: the very roots of the word *liturgy* mean "a work of the people." How does liturgy, or personal prayer with others, differ from personal prayer alone? Liturgy, the prayer of the church, communicates through the language of ritual. Liturgical prayer may be described as ritual prayer in community.

Engaging in Ritual

Perhaps the word "ritual" is a scare word, conjuring up images of boredom and tedium. With many of our public rituals such may indeed be the case. We are relieved when they come to a speedy conclusion. In reality the problem is not with ritual activity in itself, but rather with our ability or inability to identify with and enter into the ritual celebration.

Look at some nonreligious examples of ritual celebration. The opening of the Olympic Games is an example of a kind of international ritual engaging the community of nations. Rituals are always group or community activities. In your own life you may celebrate rituals as members of a family (birthday party, Thanksgiving Day), in school (graduation), at work (retirement party), or in the civic arena (inauguration of a newly-elected official, Fourth of July).

What does it mean to celebrate ritual? Ritual spells out in word and action the meaning of a given experience in our lives—another year of life for someone we love (birthday), the completion of academic studies and the beginning of a career (graduation), the retirement of a colleague, the start of a new administration for a public official. We spell out in word and action the meaning of an experience in such a way that the ritual both expresses the experience and, at the same time, deepens it.

Rituals express, capture, and frame an already existing experience. For example, the ceremonial opening of the Olympic Games frames the experience of the youth of the world competing on the plain of athletics rather than on the field of battle. At the same time the celebration of the ritual also deepens,

6

intensifies, and enlarges the experience. As a result of the opening ceremony and the ensuing contests, the experience of the solidarity among nations and the hope for world peace is enlarged and deepened. Ritual both expresses and transforms the meaning of the experience celebrated. The experience, of course, had to be there in the first instance or there would be nothing to celebrate. There would be no opening of the Olympic Games if the athletes did not come together from all over the globe to compete. At the same time, the celebration changed and transformed the meaning of the experience, raising it to a new plateau.

Christian Rituals

The particular experiences we celebrate in our Christian ritual celebrations are the experiences of the paschal mystery, *Jesus Christ crucified and risen*. Liturgy does not celebrate abstract ideas or themes; it celebrates saving events. More specifically, we celebrate the ongoing presence of God saving us through Jesus Christ in the power of the Holy Spirit. God's redemptive plan stretches back to the creation of the world when God created us in order to share with us divine life and love. His saving love continued through the covenants of the Old Testament and reached a definitive climax in the life and work of Jesus Christ who suffered, died for us, and rose from the dead.

The experience we celebrate in Christian ritual not only recalls the past but also looks to the future as we await Jesus' coming in glory. Moreover, our ritual has a very real connection to the present, where the whole sweep of God's saving purpose is expressed and made present in the actions of the liturgy into which we can enter. Saint Paul described the desired goal of liturgical prayer as "the life I live now is not my own; Christ is living in me" (Gal 2:20).

As in nonreligious rituals where the experience comes before the celebration, so too the experience of God's gracious presence in our lives precedes the celebration of Christian ritual or the sacraments. Liturgy enables Christians to frame the experience of the paschal mystery as it impacts on the life of the members of the church at decisive moments. For example, the process of Christian initiation, the experience of coming to faith and conversion in the Christian church, is ritualized in the sacraments of initiation (baptism, confirmation, eucharist). Likewise, the experience of what it means to be church gathered together finds expression in Sunday Mass. At the same time, the very celebration of the sacraments brings the paschal mystery to a new stage of completion in us as we find ourselves transformed into Christians by the initiation sacraments or incorporated more thoroughly into the Body of Christ, the church, through our participation in the Lord's Supper.

In order to understand liturgical prayer properly and appreciate its place in our lives, we need a healthy regard for ritual activity, for this is how the liturgy works as Christian religious ritual. We need to identify the experience, whether it be, for example, the love of a man and a woman (marriage) or serious illness afflicting a Christian (anointing of the sick). We identify the experience we are celebrating and then trust the ritual's dynamics to achieve their goal.

Ritual Dynamics

What are some of these ritual dynamics, the characteristics of liturgical prayer? We shall consider three: 1) liturgical prayer is rich in meaning; 2) the shape of liturgy consists of a balance between a recurring patterns and a need for flexibility; and 3) in liturgy the whole person worships.

First of all, a liturgical prayer accomplishes little in terms of concrete measurable results. It is, however, rich in meaning if we are to discover our true identity as a Christian people united to God in covenant through the merits of Jesus Christ. Liturgical prayer then is best entered into with an attitude of timelessness, as if we are "wasting time with God."

Liturgy is akin to a sense of wonder in today's world. In earlier times people could look at the universe and see the creation of a caring God who looks after the divine handiwork. Today in a more technological age the universe is viewed more as a chaos or confusion into which we have to introduce order. Look at the way we treat our natural environment!

Playfulness is important both to life and to our ritual worship. At times we seem to have lost a sense of playfulness: even vacations seem like work! G. Sheehan has written: "Without play, work is labor, sex is lust, religion is rules. Play itself becomes exercise. With play, work becomes craft, sex becomes love. Religion becomes the freedom to be a child in the Kingdom."

Another way of saying the same thing is to observe that liturgical prayer has more to do with an intuitive-receptive approach to life, one that delights in story-telling, symbol-making, art, and music. Some call this "left-handed thinking" which is controlled by the opposite or right hemisphere of the brain. This mode is in contrast to a more active intellectual approach to reality which seeks to plan, program, and organize. Such "right-handed thinking," controlled by the left hemisphere of the brain, is highly prized in today's computerized society. We actually need both approaches—receptive intuitive (left-handed) and active intellectual (right-handed)—in order to survive as persons, as a society, and as a church. Without planning and programming, we would all perish. Nevertheless, the appeal of liturgical prayer is more definitely suited to the intuitive-receptive mode of human consciousness, an important part of our lives that needs to be cultivated and encouraged.

Balance of Pattern and Flexibility

A second feature of liturgical prayer is the balance between a recurring pattern (continuity) which may be formal and repetitious, and a flexibility (discontinuity) which provides for various options. For example, a birthday party without the cake, candles, and song would not be one. Such a recurring pattern is necessary to reassure participants that they are indeed celebrating a birthday. Yet if the party is too formal or structured with no place for spontaneity, it could become as oppressive and burdensome as a military drill.

Our liturgy of the Mass and sacraments contains a recurring pattern with which people can relate and feel comfortable. Formality and repetition are not always hindrances to celebration. At the same time the rites have a variety of options built in so that the celebration can be adapted to the needs of a given worshiping community; for example, manner of song, choice of prayer texts, ritual actions, and so on.

In any assembling of people there is an opening and a closing. For example, a graduation ceremony has a distinct beginning or calling the people together as well as a distinct moment of closure and dismissal. Services of liturgical prayer also have an introductory or gathering rite and a dismissal and blessing. What is unique to Christian ritual is the public proclamation of the word of God, the public reading of the Bible, as proclaimed in the church. More specifically, there is the reading of Scripture, a response of silent prayer of a psalm from the Bible, and a prayer which sums up our response. The service of the word is usually followed by a symbolic action, whether this be a baptism, eucharist, or some other sacrament, in which, for example, Jesus washes us in the waters of baptism or nourishes us with the sacrament of his Body and Blood. Word and action are the central components of every liturgical prayer.

Total Involvement

A third characteristic of liturgical prayer is that the whole person worships. We are not a head on stilts! Worship engages the entire person as God has created and redeemed us. We worship with our minds, our hearts, our memory, our imagination, our feelings, our bodiliness, our masculinity and femininity, as members of a worshiping community or church. Liturgy is not just something we say or hear as isolated individuals: it is an activity we do as church, the Body of Christ. More specifically, there are at least eleven different actions we do in the liturgy, actions which engage the whole person in community whereby we as church exercise our share in the general priesthood of the faithful given us in baptism. Let's look at each separately.

10

Preparing. The best remote preparation for liturgical prayer is a sincere effort to live a Christian life and to cultivate sound habits of personal prayer. The best proximate preparation is to come to church with attitudes of mind and heart that expect something to happen, something good which can change our lives. And we all have a responsibility to contribute actively to what does happen according to our different roles or vocations.

Singing. Music and song are essential as we gather for liturgical prayer. It is not so much a question of liturgical music but of helping to create a musical liturgy. Catholics are only gradually recovering a tradition of participated song after many faltering efforts. Can we hear ourselves singing or are we just moving our lips? Do we allow ourselves to be moved by the beautiful singing and music of others?

Saying Prayers Together. Liturgy is praying prayers together. Our vocal participation is important. In addition to the dialogue between God and us which makes up all prayer, liturgical prayer which engages the community of the church also involves a dialogue between the congregation and the priest and other ministers as we answer the responses. Our "And also with you" and "Thanks be to God" are important.

Listening. We listen to God speaking to us when Sacred Scripture is proclaimed. It is helpful to know the readings in advance in order to prepare ourselves. How do I perceive God's call in my life? What is God saying to me? What is God calling me to?

Reflection and Silent Prayer. Liturgy is not just ceaseless action. There are times for reflection and silent prayer built into our liturgical prayer, especially after the sermon and after holy communion. These periods are not passive, empty silences, but periods of active silence filled with the presence of God. We have an opportunity to make our own what is happening to us.

Movement and Gestures. We worship with our bodies. Consider the postures we assume: standing is more attentive, sitting is more for listening, kneeling for repentance and adoration. We make gestures which are expressive of reverence for the mystery we celebrate: bows, genuflections, the sign of the cross. We walk in processions when called upon to present the

11

gifts or when it is time to share the eucharist at communion.
The whole person worships God in liturgical prayer.

Watching. We are not idle spectators but interested and involved participants paying attention to what is happening or
to what we create in liturgical action. We should be aware of
the environment of worship, the liturgical space, the decorative
art, the actions and movements of the liturgy. We should consider the lighting, colors, vestments, or special clothes worn
by some of the ministers. Most importantly, we should pay
attention to our brothers and sisters participating with us. Attentive watching can lead us more deeply into the mystery of
God as we celebrate our faith.

Interceding. Most of the prayers at Mass are prayers of petition: we ask God for the blessing we seek. We also ask God's
help for the needs of the universal church, for public authorities and the salvation of the world, for those oppressed by any
need, and for the local community. If our liturgy is to be
authentic, there must be a close correlation between our prayer
together and our desire as the Body of Christ to work for a
better world of justice and peace.

Thanking. One of the oldest words for the Lord's Supper, the
Mass, is *eucharist*. Eucharist means praise and thanksgiving.
We give thanks and praise especially during the great thanksgiving or eucharistic prayer found at the heart of the Mass
when the bread and wine are changed into the sacrament of
the Lord's Body and Blood.

Offering. The Mass is a memorial sacrifice. We recall and
make present the total gift of Christ given to us on Calvary
when he died for us. To this we give the gift of ourselves,
responding to the deepest longings of the human heart to give
ourselves to a union with God. Our responses of "Amen" are
our act of offering, our dedication, our recommitment.

Receiving/Accepting. We receive the word of God proclaimed
and preached. We accept the Gift of gifts, the Bread of Life and
the Cup of eternal salvation at communion. In the last analysis,
everything is gift, as Saint Paul reminds us:

12

I repeat, it is owing to his favor that salvation is yours through faith. This is not your own doing, it is God's gift; neither is it a reward for anything you have accomplished, so let no one pride himself on it. We are truly his handiwork, created in Christ Jesus to lead the life of good deeds which God prepared for us in advance. (Eph 2:8–10)

Making Worship Work

CHAPTER 2

Cheerless faces! People coming in late and leaving early. Young people who do not want to be there at all. Children whose crying during Mass is tolerated as if the liturgy were some kind of prerecorded media presentation one would view on television with no disruption to the communication process. If there is any bright spot, it is occasionally the homily, certainly not the ritual event as a whole. Is this too grim a picture? Make no mistake about it, the Roman Catholic Church has made enormous strides in a long-neglected and welcome revamping of its liturgy. Nonetheless, public enemy number one of the liturgical renewal is a sense of boredom, of tedium, which grips many parishes on Sunday.

What is desperately needed today is a feel for good worship. Unfortunately we often settle for less. For example, there still persists a juridical notion that liturgy is something imposed from on high, in an overly pyramidal conception of church: "Can I do it?" "Do I have to do it?" Sometimes the most important question is the last one posed: "Will it be pastorally beneficial?" Or again, in some quarters there flourishes an extrinsic approach—as if liturgy were something out there that goes on relentlessly, whether or not you are a part of it. At other times

15

liturgy is seen as a machine: liturgy *works*, is effective, no matter how it is performed—almost to a complete neglect of the basic dynamics of human communication.

What we need is a solid grasp of the inner meaning of worship. This implies an awareness of the living tradition of the church continued in the revised rites. It means a lively sense of sign and symbol: sacraments are not things but *graced human actions* involving such basic elements as a baptismal bath, an anointing with oil, a shared eucharistic meal. And all of this should express and reveal our inner faith and spirituality as we respond to the dialogue of prayer initiated by God. What we are really talking about is liturgical ownership. After years of intensive liturgical revision, we have built ourselves a new house of liturgical rites. Now we have to claim it as our home. Then we will be able to enter more fully into the experience of worship.

We could begin by rereading the Constitution on the Sacred Liturgy (1963), the first fruits of the Second Vatican Council, and bring to life, by experiencing them, the many principles which inspire the present reform. When the Constitution states that the liturgy expresses and forms the church, "church" does not means some ideal abstraction, but a flesh and blood community of believers who make up the local church or parish. When it speaks of the sanctification of persons "signified by signs perceptible to the senses" and "effected in a way which corresponds to each of these signs" (no. 7), the intent is that sacraments *work* insofar as they are good symbols. The signing and effecting go together as two sides of the same coin.

When the Constitution teaches that normally faith and conversion should precede liturgical celebration (no. 9), it is anticipating the impact of the recently restored Rite of Christian Initiation of Adults, although for now we shall often have to settle for a kind of concurrent evangelization for Christians already sacramentalized, but not yet brought to some manner of adult interiorization or conversion. When we hear that the liturgy, more specifically, the eucharistic liturgy, is the "source and summit of Christian life" (no. 10), this presupposes something going on in parish life besides Sunday Mass—in terms of Christian community, catechesis, and social outreach.

When the Vatican II document stresses the necessity of personal dispositions (no. 11) and an extension of the spiritual life beyond liturgical participation (no. 12), this is a constant reminder of the absolute need for times of private daily prayer and for coming together to pray on occasions that are not eucharistic. When servers, readers, musicians, and other ministers are accorded a genuine liturgical function (no. 29), this challenges us to an ongoing formation and motivation of all ministries—beginning with the basic mission of the church which became ours on the day of our baptism.

The overriding aim of all liturgical renewal, however, has been the "full, conscious, and active participation of the people" (no. 14). If the primary liturgical need today is a feel for good worship, a grasp of the inner meaning of liturgical prayer, let us explore more in detail how God is communicating with us in the liturgy—involving our entire being, our total humanity. This is nothing more yet nothing less than an extension of the meaning of the incarnation of the Son of God as it has profoundly marked our relationship with God. God wants our liturgical participation to be a graced human experience, a religious experience, an encounter with the Father through Christ in the Spirit in the community of the church. The experience of worship engages our minds, memory, imagination, feelings, body, heart, masculinity/femininity, other people. The whole person worships.

We Worship with Our *Minds*

Perhaps this aspect of liturgical communication has been overstressed in the past, as if the liturgy were a cerebral exercise with a lot of words reminiscent of a classroom. We do need a basic familiarity with the structure of the Mass and the sacraments. We should be aware of the scriptural readings in advance, which can be listed in the parish bulletin for our prayerful preparation. We should also know why we come together in the first place—for the Sunday eucharist is the very center of the unity of the church. But most especially, we should understand the particular way that the mystery of God, Father, Son, and Spirit, is communicated to us—a manner of communication which runs much deeper than mere rational discourse, namely, through story and through rite.

The word of God is the story of God's gracious dealings with us, God's desire to form a covenant, to enter into a communion of life with us, to be our God. Another page in this story of salvation history is written every time the good news of the Gospel is proclaimed. The evocative power of story-telling and biography is very popular in catechetics and religious education these days. It is as old as the parables of Jesus and could well provide a renewed impetus for preaching: divine truths communicated in a human way through images and metaphors, so that we can grasp and retain them better. And the most important message underlying the story-telling of the liturgy of the word is: our God is in love with us.

In addition to story-telling, the rite is the other way that the Christian mystery is communicated. Maybe ritual activity is not receiving rave reviews in contemporary life. Yet now and then occurs a moving non-church ritual—such as the tribute given to the late Yankee baseball great, Thurman Munson—which causes people to sit back, pay attention, and become emotionally involved. What we do when we celebrate any ritual is to spell out the meaning of a given experience in word and action—in a way that expresses and deepens and prolongs this experience. The capacity crowd at Yankee Stadium on that warm August evening, stimulated by Cardinal Cooke's invocation and Robert Merrill's rendition of "America the Beautiful," was spelling out in word and action the experience of appreciation and farewell to a well-respected player. The scoreboard flashing various designs and the crowd spontaneously chanting "Thurman" contributed both to express and to deepen this tribute.

The fact of the matter is that liturgy is Christian religious ritual. The particular experience that our Christian liturgy expresses and brings about is our incorporation into the saving paschal mystery of Jesus crucified and risen. It is the paradoxical Christian answer to the meaning of human existence: you win by seemingly losing, or better put, you win by loving with an unselfish love. And this love is itself a gift of God, enabling us to imitate Jesus' own self-offering.

We Worship with Our *Memory*

Both the corporate memory of the church—*anamnesis* is the technical term for this—and our own personal affective bond with Christ are brought to life when we remember Jesus in the memorial sacrifice we call the Mass, when like the disciples at Emmaus we recognize him in the breaking of the bread. This is the way Jesus asked to be remembered as is recorded in the oldest account we possess of the Lord's Supper: "Do this in remembrance of me."

We Worship with Our *Imagination*

Worship is an activity quite apart from what occupies us during the rest of the week: hours spent at work, doing household chores, completing school assignments, and the like. Liturgy simply defies measurement in quantitative terms. It is more akin to wonder, contemplation, fantasy, play. Worship is a different way of being present to God and to others, and yet it is the most important activity we can engage in. It has to do with what is most real—the celebration of our relationship with God wherein we find our deepest identity. Romano Guardini put it well when he remarked that liturgy is low in concrete purpose but very rich in meaning.

We Worship with Our *Feelings*

Although there may be dry periods, such as we experience in our personal prayer alone, normally we should enjoy church. We often labor under an unhealthy confusion between fasting and feasting. As a result, we reduce our liturgical celebrations to a form of asceticism, as if the more it hurts the better

19

it is for us and the more glory is given to God! What kind of an image of God lurks behind this caricature, as if God calls us together in order to be bored in the divine presence! There is a very real place for self-discipline in Christian life—the contrast between fasting and feasting could be more pronounced—but the liturgy should be a joyous celebration of faith, giving us strength and hope to continue on our journey toward God as followers of Jesus.

We worship with our feelings. This is one reason why there is music in liturgy, with its rich power to create a mood. Usually we sing only when we are happy or otherwise deeply moved by something. An awareness of emotions and feelings can also unlock for us the great beauty of the use of psalms in worship. This poetry from the Hebrew Scriptures treats of such fundamental concerns as: survival, struggle, birth, death, life, fear, darkness, work, rest.

We Worship with Our *Body*

Consider the processions at Mass. Liturgical ministers ought to be aware that processions are a kind of dance form—the movement of the body should be in rhythm with the music. Some of the processions involve the congregation: for example, the procession of gifts and the reception of communion. The communion procession is more than just standing in line to receive the sacrament of the Lord's Body and Blood.

We use gestures in worship. The very beginning of Mass opens with the sign of the cross, a reminder of our baptism when we were first marked with the sign of Christ. We bow. We genuflect. We exchange the sign of peace (which is to be conveyed with great care and reverence for persons—not as a political campaigner working over the crowds). Furthermore, our varying postures play a natural, important role in worship. Standing is the basic liturgical posture. Sitting is more for attentive listening and relaxation. Kneeling is the original penitential posture. All these would make more sense with a seating arrangement more flexible than stationary pews.

We Worship with Our *Hearts*

We have all experienced moments when the general intercessions (when not a string of pious exhortations recapping the homily) provoke a sense of cosmic awareness that we are praying for all men and women, who suddenly become our brothers and sisters. At other times a reverent and festive eucharistic prayer, especially when enriched by the standing posture of the congregation, who mingle sung acclamations with the prayer, results in a feeling of awe and wonder, praise and thanksgiving, welling up from the heart. We worship from the heart. This is why we call the Mass a sacrifice: we recall and, through the power of the Spirit, the Father makes present Jesus' dying and rising—to which we say "Amen" by offering together all that we have and are. The Mass becomes our sacrifice to the extent that it is accompanied by our own commitment and rededication as we try to let God love us the way God wants to love us.

We Worship as *Men and Women*

We are sexed beings, male or female, to the very core of our personalities. In a very male-dominated Roman liturgy, we may have forgotten the more centered, intuitive, feminine approach to reality and to God. At the very least, it is time to clean up the sexist language which permeates our revised rites and to use a way of speaking and praying more inclusive of both men and women.

Worship Involves *Other People*

Indeed, this is the very reason why we rely upon ritual symbols—which would not be so necessary in our personal, individual prayer. This is the special characteristic of liturgical prayer: it is prayer *together*, the *public* worship of the church. The ultimate purpose why bread and wine are changed into the Body and Blood of Christ is to bring about a further change, a transformation of ourselves into his Body which is the

21

church. Not only the presiding celebrant and liturgical ministers, but every member of the worshiping assembly has a responsibility to God and to each other to become intrinsically interested and involved in the celebration of our worship. As Paul said: "Be filled with the Spirit, addressing one another in psalms and hymns and inspired songs" (Eph 5:18). We owe this to each other. We support and carry one another in faith. The first problem is not getting other people to come to church—but rather to make our liturgy a genuine religious experience for us who are already there and thirsting for more.

CHAPTER 3

Liturgy and Social Consciousness

Speaking at Saint Peter's College on the first draft of the bishops' pastoral letter on the economy, Governor Mario Cuomo of New York had this to say:

> They have called us to God's work in this bleeding, broken, imperfect world of ours, reminding us that our faith doesn't end at the Communion rail, that it must extend into the mean streets of Jersey City and New York and Chicago—anywhere where our brothers and sisters go without work or enough to eat, some without even a roof over their heads.[1]

In effect, the governor was cautioning his audience against a split consciousness, as if faith were one thing, economics another; as if we could differentiate what we do on Sunday from the way we lead our lives during the rest of the week. To paraphrase the remarks made by John Haughey, S.J.: we are challenged to a unitary consciousness whose center is beyond

1. *The Catholic Free Press*, Worcester, 31 May 1985.

23

oneself; we are called to discover the whole Christ, to recover a horizontal transcendence.[2] And the most promising way of developing a unitary consciousness that integrates our Christian commitment with the whole of reality is through the eucharist. Here are some concrete suggestions as to how the celebration of Mass can promote a unitary consciousness as applied to the liturgical environment, ministries, and the Order of Mass.

Liturgical Environment

The liturgical environment should promote a people-oriented, not a thing-oriented liturgy. Consider these excerpts from the United States Bishops' "Environment and Art in Catholic Worship." "Among the symbols with which liturgy deals, none is more important than this assembly of believers" (no. 28). "The most powerful experience of the sacred is found in the celebration and the persons celebrating, that is, it is found in the action of the assembly: the living word, the living gestures, the living sacrifice, the living meal" (no. 29).

In other words, the church at worship, the liturgical assembly, is the fundamental symbol or sacrament. The church building serves as the *domus ecclesiae*, quite literally, "the house of the church," which is a living community of faith. The liturgical environment should be so designed as to enable the church to be church, to be what it is supposed to be—the people of God, the Body of Christ.

Generally speaking, we need five spaces in the assembly area for this to happen.

Congregational Space. The seating, flexible seating if possible, should allow the worshipers to see each other as they gather around the table of the word and the table of the eucharist. We no longer renovate only sanctuaries, but the total worship space.

Movement Space. God's people need movement space to take

2. During his lecture series, "The Eucharist and the Economy," given at Seton Hall, Spring 1985.

part in processions: entrance procession; the gospel procession (Alleluia), now possible with a gospel book; the procession with the gifts of bread and wine; and the procession to receive the Body and Blood of Christ at communion.

Baptismal Space. The space for celebrating this gateway sacrament to the Christian life should allow room for people to stand around a permanent font large enough to enable a water bath by immersion, as the revised initiation rites recommend.

Choir Space. The ministry of music should be located in the assembly area up front so that the choir's ministry is not only heard but seen as it leads the musical participation of the assembly.

Sanctuary Space. This space provides for the principal liturgical appointments of the table/altar, the lectern or ambo, and the presidential chair. The Blessed Sacrament is best reserved in a separate eucharistic chapel. This arrangement allows for the dynamic unfolding of the presence of Christ at Mass (gathered assembly, word, presider, eucharistic elements) to take place in the main assembly area, while at the same time promoting a place of meditation before the reserved sacrament at times other than Mass (Environment and Art, no. 78).

One might also plead that the church building be accessible for the physically handicapped, by ramps or, if necessary, elevators. Also important are gathering spaces for the parishioners to share and to be one with one another before and after the eucharistic liturgy. This approach to a people-oriented, not a thing-oriented, liturgy is a beginning toward recovering a horizontal transcendence, a unitary consciousness where liturgy and life come together. "They devoted themselves to the apostles' instruction and the communal life, to the breaking of bread and the prayers" (Acts 2:42).

Ministries

Who celebrates the eucharist? The whole people of God: "a chosen race, a royal priesthood, a holy nation, a people set apart" (1 Pt 2:9). The Mass is not the priest's private prerogative or monopoly apart from the people he serves. The General

Instruction to the Roman Missal, when speaking of the eucharistic prayer, puts it this way: "The meaning of the prayer is that the whole congregation joins Christ in acknowledging the works of God and in offering the sacrifice" (no. 54). It is not a question of those who give, those who receive; those who are active, those who are passive. All give/receive, are active/passive at different times according to a diversity of roles and ministries. This applies to all designated ministers, ordained and nonordained: they are there to facilitate the worship experience of the total assembly animated by the Holy Spirit to praise God.

Ministry does not mean doing things for people or to people; ministry means doing things with people. Ministry begins with hospitality, which Eugene Walsh feels is the best English rendering of the Greek *agape* (unselfish love). Here are some specific examples:

- priests who greet you at the door when you arrive, not waiting until the end when you leave! Presiders who are able to combine prayerful reverence with gracious hospitality;
- ushers who are true ministers of hospitality, whose whole demeanor says "Welcome! We are glad you are with us!"
- ministers of music who provide a warmup that makes people comfortable and invites their participation;
- good readers who are eager to communicate and share God's word;
- eucharistic ministers whose friendly reverence invites you to make your personal profession of faith in the whole Christ: "The Body of Christ." "Amen." "The Blood of Christ." "Amen."

Hospitality means inclusiveness in the liturgy. The selection of particular ministries should be representative of the racial, ethnic, and social makeup of the parish. Inclusiveness means that special attention be given to the much neglected and underdeveloped ministry of women. Archbishop Gerety gave this directive several years ago in his pastoral letter on women in the church.

> Religious and lay women should be invited and encouraged to participate in every role of the liturgical life of the community which the Church permits. This includes membership on liturgy committees, service as readers and commentators, as special ministers of the Eucharist and leaders of song, as ushers and greeters. May our worshipping communities more clearly express their true identity as brothers and sisters in Christ. May our liturgical celebrations witness to the wide variety of the gifts of the Spirit in women and men gathered together in praise and thanksgiving.[3]

Inclusiveness also means that our language is nonsexist. A bit of sensitivity will be needed in converting "brothers" to "brothers and sisters," "sons" to "sons and daughters," "men" to "men and women," and the generic "man" or "mankind" to "humanity," the "human race," or "human family."

The Order of Mass

Here are some adaptations, or better, shifts of emphasis, that could be made to the celebration of the Order of Mass so as to bring about a more unitary consciousness, a horizontal transcendence, a wedding of liturgy and life.

Gathering Rites. Jesus tells us, "Where two or three are gathered in my name, there am I in their midst" (Mt 18:20). The purpose of the introductory rites is to gather the people together in the Lord. Usually we proceed from praying alone (one enters a quiet church; it is disrespectful to talk) to praying together (participational liturgical prayer). Oftentimes, however, the result is more a collectivity of individual persons at prayer rather than the corporate prayer of the church. The suggestion is to begin by creating a sense of being together and from there to move on to praying together. I have personally

3. *The Advocate,* 11 February 1981.

27

seen this work, for example, at a Mass in the Oakland, California, cathedral. The people arrive early, happy to see one another. Without becoming boisterous, there is a quiet conviviality. The priests go through the church greeting the people, chatting with them. As the time for the eucharist draws near, the leader of song introduces the celebration, a choir motet follows to set the mood for worship, and the entrance procession begins. The change is a subtle but important one: from praying alone/praying together to being together/praying together.

Liturgy of the Word. Christ speaks when the word is proclaimed. There is no need to seat the readers in the sanctuary area; rather, have them come forward out of the assembly at the proper time. The proclamation of Scripture is an act of story-telling: the greatest story ever told, the story of God's self-communication to us, God's saving intervention into history, and his presence in our lives here and now. Have the readers pick up the lectionary and read it with feeling, affectivity, and devotion. Preachers might also reflect upon their ecclesiology (does the church exist for the self-nurture of its members only, or does it rather seek to empower its members for a mission in the world?) and eschatology (are there the two worlds of religion and life, or rather one in which God, the driving force of history, and the kingdom at work in the world are what are most real?). The general intercessions, which are envisioned to address the real concerns and needs of people everywhere, are best carefully and prayerfully prepared from the lectionary and the daily newspaper.

Liturgy of the Eucharist. Christ is present in the eucharistic forms of bread and wine. The preparation of gifts should emphasize bread and wine as robust symbols. Sometimes one finds a curious tendency to resort to a kind of "ecclesiastical thinness" rather than employing good human symbols capable of conveying transcendence. We should also be mindful of gifts for the poor. And let us not be shy about the money taken up in the collection (preferably presented together with the sacramental gifts), lest we fall prey to a kind of dualism. There is nothing wrong with money, expressive of human goods and services; the question at issue in the bishops' pastoral on the economy is the use to which money is put.

Invite the people to stand during the eucharistic prayer. Standing is the original posture of the Christian assembly at prayer, especially the prayer of praise and thanksgiving. Furthermore, when the faithful people of God are kneeling before the standing presiding celebrant, one is left with the impression that the priest alone is active and that the people are reduced to a very passive role. Sung acclamations could enrich the people's participation as would also a greater variety of officially approved eucharistic prayers.

Nowhere is the ecclesiology of the worshiping community more visibly manifest than during the sharing of the eucharist during the communion rite. Do the people sing during the communion procession as they come forward to receive the sacrament of the unity of the church? Is the sacrament of the Lord's Body and Blood shared under both kinds at every Mass, a provision our American bishops fought long and hard to obtain? Are there enough eucharistic ministers to make this possible? Are the eucharistic ministers dismissed early (after the prayer after communion) to bring the eucharist to the extended assembly confined to their homes?

Dismissal. The dismissal is where the presence of Christ comes full circle. Gathered in his name, nourished by his word and the sacrament of his Body and Blood, the faithful people of God have been transformed into his Body which is the church. Actually, this is the reason for the change of the bread and wine into the Body and Blood of Christ (transubstantiation), so that we, in the words of Saint Augustine, might "be what we see and receive what we are" (transfinalization). We are the Body of Christ, the dynamic mystical unity that exists between Jesus the Head and we his members. What was first in the order of intention (church as Body of Christ) is last in the order of execution, brought about through reception of the eucharistic Body of Christ. As church, as Body of Christ, we are sent forth, dismissed, with a mission in the world to work for justice and peace as constitutive elements of the Gospel.

We have been considering ways in which the celebration of

Mass can promote a unitary consciousness, bringing faith and justice together so that what we do on Sunday morning has a direct bearing on our lives during the rest of the week. Perhaps the biggest obstacle to all this is an individualistic, consumer society espousing independence, whereas the church is preaching the interdependence of the members of the Body of Christ. There is a further conflict of attitudes that one can bring to the worshiping assembly. "What am I getting out of it?" needs to be replaced by "What do I bring to the assembly? How can I support and sustain the other members of the Body of Christ?" This basic Christian attitude must also contend with the constant media bombardment tempting us to believe that "Happiness is found in buying our products!" whereas one hour a week we have a chance to express what we know in our heart of hearts is true: "Happiness is found in being for others."

Liturgy and Catechesis

CHAPTER 4

For a long time liturgy and catechesis have been feuding like two estranged partners whose marriage was on the rocks. Angry recriminations have been hurled back and forth. Liturgists accused catechists of not understanding the nature of liturgy, of manipulating worship for didactic purposes as if it were a kind of catechetical tool. Catechists responded in turn that liturgists were too rubrical, too rigid, too unyielding and inflexible, not really in touch with reality, sometimes calling them "litniks." In this estranged marriage there were sharp exchanges, people using the same words but investing them with different meanings. For example, what do we mean by "evangelization" or "catechesis"? Liturgists need to know that catechists have moved beyond the classroom model of instruction toward a more holistic formation process, whether this be called catechesis or Christian religious education.

This marital situation between catechesis and liturgy deteriorated so sharply that a counselor was needed. A marriage counselor was found in the person of Pope John Paul II in his apostolic exhortation "Catechesis in Our Time," promulgated in 1979, particularly in paragraph 23. Like any good marriage

counselor, he first of all attempts to settle down the two partners and to show how much they need one another. He writes:

> Catechesis is intrinsically linked with the whole of liturgical and
> sacramental activity, for it is in the sacraments, especially in the
> Eucharist, that Christ Jesus works in fullness for the transforma-
> tion of human beings.[1]

Now the next thing any marriage counselor would want to
do is to explore the nature of the relationship in the past, the
family history, the genesis of their coming together in the first
place, what catechesis and liturgy have in common. John Paul
II continues, telling us that this recent rift between catechesis
and liturgy was not always there:

> In the early Church, the catechumenate and preparation for the
> sacraments of baptism and eucharist were the same thing.

Perhaps an historical commentary is in order here. Originally
catechesis and liturgy were two sides of the same coin of Christian initiation: the multi-dimensional process of coming to faith
and conversion called the catechumenate. The adult
catechumenate flourished in the early church, especially from
the third to the fifth century. What subsequently happened
was a disintegration of the process of adult initiation. The
catechumenate was dismantled by the sixth century, and the
church settled into the practice of baptizing infants exclusively.
At the same time the sacramental unity of baptism, confirmation, and first eucharist—originally celebrated as a continuum
in sequential order at the Easter Vigil—was lost. The initiation
sacraments were no longer celebrated together at the Easter
Vigil but at different times. Still later the sequence became dis-
torted so that the order was no longer baptism, confirmation,

1. John Paul II, *Catechesi tradendae* (16 October 1979), reprinted in Austin
Flannery, ed., *Vatican Council II: More Post-Conciliar Documents* (Northport,
NY: Costello Publishing Co., 1982) 776. Paragraph 23, cited throughout this
chapter, has provided the inspiration for my treatment of this subject.

and eucharist, but rather baptism, eucharist, and confirmation—the situation we have inherited today.

Here are the results. Catechesis became deritualized into religious education of a classroom variety. The emphasis was on the catechism itself, especially during the period after the Council of Trent in the sixteenth century. During the whole post-Tridentine counter-reformation period, for Protestants and Catholics alike, the concentration was on the catechism. For example, Martin Luther published a longer and a shorter catechism. The catechism reprinted in the *Book of Common Prayer* was intended to prepare candidates for confirmation in the Anglican Communion. Roman Catholics had the *Catechism of the Council of Trent* and, for the church in America since the last century, the well-known *Baltimore Catechism*. The compelling motivation seemd to be the more you knew, the better and more holy you would become. Consequently, baptism was reduced to a kind of exorcistic rite removing original sin and inducting the baptized into the proletariat of the faithful as the bottom of the ecclesiastical pyramid. And finally, the catechumenate in a sense never really disappeared, but rather migrated to novitiates and seminaries where the elite Christians, the religious and clergy, were formed.

Pope John Paul continues, pointing the way to the future reconciliation and reunion of catechesis and liturgy, which is found in the Rite of Christian Initiation of Adults (1972) with its restored catechumenate.

> Although in the countries that have long been Christian, the Church has changed her practice in this field, the catechumenate has never been abolished; on the contrary, it is experiencing a renewal in those countries and is abundantly practiced in the young missionary countries.

The RCIA, Liturgy, and Catechesis

How does the RCIA help bring about a reconciliation between liturgy and catechesis? It does so in several ways.

One way is the *interplay of the four periods and the three stages or steps.* The formation periods of evangelization, catechumenate, Lenten enlightenment, and the Easter mystagogy are hinged together—"hinged" is the best way to describe this relationship—by the liturgical steps which are respectively the liturgical celebrations of the rites of entry, election, and the highlight of all, the initiation sacraments at the Easter Vigil. It is necessary to see how the periods and stages fit together. The steps are not liturgical hoops the candidates jump through to keep going. Rather, these rites celebrate the different stages of progress in the catechumenal catechesis which then impel the candidates into the next period.

A second way is to see how the RCIA and the restored catechumenate have brought about a reconciliation of catechesis and liturgy is to recognize that the *privileged moment of formal catechesis occurs on Sundays* during the liturgy of the word at Mass and the subsequent dismissal of the catechumens where that word is broken open and shared by the catechists and sponsors. This is the most important catechesis of the week for the convert, and its content should be drawn from the readings of the Sunday lectionary, not from some kind of canned program you buy in a textbook.

Still a third way how catechesis and liturgy come together is found in the *recovery of mystagogy during the Easter season*, during which the neophytes reflect back with the local church on the meaning of their initiatory experience and the mysteries of baptism, confirmation, and the eucharist in their lives. In the mystagogical catechesis called for, of which there are abundant examples from Ambrose, John Chrysostom, Cyril of Jerusalem, and others in the ancient church, catechesis once again becomes a path leading into the liturgical life and culminating in the eucharist.

The biggest contribution of all, however, which the restored RCIA has made to bring about a re-wedding of catechesis and liturgy is that it has helped us to see that the connecting link between the two is *evangelization leading to conversion.* Evangelization leading to conversion is what those two alienated marriage partners have in common, what unites them in a common purpose. This is also what the church is about: to proclaim the

34

Gospel of Jesus Christ calling people to faith and conversion, and to continue to sustain and nourish the faith and conversion of its members so that the church may truly be a sign of Christ's enduring presence in the world. Let's unpack this further.

Evangelization

The term evangelization admits of two meanings. A more restricted meaning of evangelization refers to the initial proclamation of the Gospel which is directed toward conversion and followed by catechesis. This is what the pre-catecumenate or evangelization period of the RCIA is about: the initial conversion which flows from the first hearing of the Gospel. But there is also a broader meaning of evangelization which Paul VI had in mind in his ground-breaking apostolic letter "Evangelization in the Modern World" (1975). The pope calls evangelization an "activity whereby the Church proclaims the Gospel, so that faith may be aroused, may unfold and may grow." This evangelization is an ongoing process within the Christian community which should happen every day and particularly in our day where there is such a pressing need for a concurrent evangelization in our churches of those already sacramentally initiated. Paul VI puts it another way when he says: "For the Church, evangelizing means bringing the Good News into all the strata of humanity, and through its influence, transforming humanity from within and making it new."[2] Evangelization thus has a restricted sense, implying the first hearing of and conversion to the Gospel, and a wider sense which is the ongoing task of the church to bring Christ to all sectors of the human situation.

Conversion

What is meant by conversion? Religious conversion is the process of falling in love with God. Christian conversion is

2. Paul VI, *Evangelii nuntiandi* (8 December 1975) par. 18, reprinted in Flannery, *Vatican Council II* 718.

experiencing the mystery of Christ crucified and risen in your life, the cross as the way to salvation. Conversion is letting the Holy Spirit take over your life. A friend of mine who experienced conversion recently described how this has impacted on his life. Before the conversion he used to ask God to do what he wanted God to do for him; he was really at the center attempting to manipulate God. Now it is all reversed: when he prays he asks God to show him where God wants him to be, where he can be for God. God is now truly the center of his life.

Conversion means that Jesus Christ is Lord not only of the big picture; but as the conversion becomes more interiorized, he becomes Lord more and more of the smaller details of this big picture. In short, he becomes the Lord of all. Jim Dunning best captures the full implications of conversion in a series of contrasts drawn from Jim Wallis' *Call to Conversion*.[3] Conversion is a movement from idols to God, from slavery to freedom, from injustice to justice, from guilt to forgiveness, from lies to truth, from darkness to light, from self to others, from death to life, from fear to hope, from control to relinquishment, from despair to joy, from wealth to simplicity, from the bomb to the cross, from alienation to reconciliation, from domination to servanthood, from anxiety to prayer, from false security to trust, from selfishness to sacrifice, from superiority to equality, from chauvinism to mutuality, from consumption to conservation, from accumulating to giving away, from hate to love of enemies, from swords to ploughshares, from individualism to community, from America first to Jesus first.

The church's mission is to be a catalyst facilitating the conversion process. In order to accomplish this mission, the church is moving away from an earlier inquiry class, lecture, school model approach in favor of a more holistic formational model. This socialization/inculturation model comprises four components, which are described in the RCIA (no. 75 in particular) as well as in the National Catechetical Directory: growth in community, apostolic outreach, catechesis, and liturgical celebration. Each deserves consideration.

3. Jim Wallis, *Call to Conversion* (New York: Harper & Row, 1981).

First of all, *growth in community:* living the Christian way together. As is clear from the history of salvation, God calls us by our first name, wants to enter into a personal relationship with us. But at the same time, God saves us as a people, a people of God, the Body of Christ. This divine revelation is at odds with an attitude of unhealthy individualism so prevalent in our society and culture today: "I did it my way," as if you almost have to apologize for ever needing the help and support of others. Maybe something of this "rugged individualism" colors our approach to God. In everything else we strive for independence, so also in our relationship with God and others. Contrasted to this is the call of Christ to be his embodiment in the world, to be the Body of Christ with a variety of gifts and ministries and charisms which need each other. Not independence as much as inter-dependence is the goal to which the church calls us. The first component of the conversion process facilitated by the church is growth in community.

The second component of the conversion process is *apostolic outreach.* Although this may be considered the very fruit of the whole conversion process, I would like to treat it here, so as to move on to consider catechesis and liturgy more explicitly. Apostolic outreach means that you are a Christian not only for yourself, but for others. The Christian is not only saved but also sent forth with a mission. The biggest shortcoming in Christian formation today at any level is a failure to instill a sense of mission, ministry, and outreach in people's lives. It is a fallacy to think we could somehow form Christians without giving them a sense of being apostles in the world. We are called to be members of a church that is a sign and instrument proclaiming the Kingdom of God in the world. It is impossible to make a strict dichotomy between our Christian commitment and our profession in the political and economic arena.

The third component of the conversion process is *catechesis.* Indeed, the whole process of conversion could be called catechesis in a wider sense. Catechist Bob Hater has described this wider sense of catechesis as an "informal catechesis" consisting of those "pastoral activities—family, prayer, speaking of God's love to a friend, community building, evangelical ac-

37

tivities, service projects, liturgy—which, even if not intended primarily to catechize, have a catechetical aspect." Normally, however, when the word "catechesis" is used, one has in mind a more formal catechesis, catechesis proper, or structured catechesis, which would be "those pastoral activities which aim at calling forth a response to the living word of God in a deliberate, intentional, and structured way." Catechesis is thus a ministry based on the word of God flowing from Scripture. In the wake of the impact biblical fundamentalism has made on so many good Catholic Christians, the biblically oriented catechesis called for by the RCIA is especially relevant today wherever the church seeks to catechize.

The fourth component of this process of evangelization leading to conversion is *liturgical celebration*. What do we do when we celebrate a liturgy? We engage in the activity of Christian religious ritual. And what is ritual activity in the first place? What we do when we celebrate any ritual is to take a given experience and spell out the meaning of this experience in word and action. We ritualize it. The ritual is not the rubric, neither is it the book: the ritual is the event of celebration. In spelling out the meaning of the experience we express the meaning that is already there; at the same time we deepen and prolong the experience. What any good ritual does is both to frame and to enlarge a given experience. An example from the nonreligious realm may help enflesh this description: for example, a presidential inauguration and all the attendant festivities. One does not just begin with a ritual; first of all you have to have an experience to ritualize. We want to spell out the meaning of this experience in word and action, capturing what it means to celebrate four years of a new administration in office. Think of rituals we celebrate at schools (e.g., graduations), family rituals (e.g., birthday parties), and ethnic customs (e.g., pageants and processions) ritually celebrated to highlight important occasions. In any ritual we begin with the experience; in our Christian religious ritual the experience we begin with is already a graced experience. In every liturgy we capture some aspect of the mystery of Christ crucified and risen, the paschal mystery at work in our lives, the mystery of the salvation of the world. In the sacraments of initiation we spell out the meaning of the experience of coming to faith and conversion in the Christian church, as experienced by adults or by children; we celebrate a transformation ritually expressed and brought about in the sacraments of baptism, confirmation, and eucharist. The experience ritualized in the Sunday eucharistic assembly is everything it means to be church, to be the Body of Christ: this is what is expressed ritually, brought about, enlarged, and transformed in the Sunday eucharistic assembly.

The implications are rich and vast. It implies there is a connecting link between life and liturgy which has to be perceived. We need to be in touch with our religious experiences. Whether we journal or simply prayerfully reflect, do not let those precious human experiences charged with divine grace go by. By being in touch with our religious experiences, we are able to see where God is at work in our lives and know that the sacraments are transforming these experiences of grace already happening. There is also a reflexive influence which transforms the experience itself, so that eventually we may be able to identify with the words of Saint Paul: "The life I live now is not my own; Christ is living in me" (Gal 2:20). There is also an implication here for the church and the renewal of its liturgy. The first phase of the liturgical renewal is coming to a close with the publication of the revised rites. However, the liturgical reform is not a question of a new library of books, but rather the renewal of the church through its liturgy. The goal of the revised rites of the church is a renewal of the very experience of being church. In terms of pastoral liturgy it comes down to this. When we celebrate the liturgy, we should be able to identify the experience we are celebrating. Why are we here? What are we doing? And at the same time we celebrate the liturgy, we should be able to trust the ritual to do its job, when celebrated well, to bring about what it is supposed to do.

Religious Imagination

Hopefully, thus far we have been able to effect something of a *rapprochement* between catechesis and liturgy through the

39

insight gleaned from the RCIA and the restored catechumenate that the connecting link between the two is evangelization leading to conversion. This holds true not only for the Christian being initiated but also for the ongoing conversion of already initiated Christians. Evangelization leading to conversion is what brings catechesis and liturgy together. But there is more. Competent marriage counselors usually suggest to couples what they can work at in order to develop further their relationship: how to improve communication, how to make the relationship more interesting and exciting for both parties. What can we suggest in terms of counseling to help this marriage a little bit along? A priority would be for both partners to pay more attention to the religious imagination.

Here is one way of looking at religious imagination. In every human person two modes of consciousness are at work, sometimes called right-handed (left brain) thinking and left-handed (right brain) thinking. John Westerhoff prefers to distinguish between an active intellectual-volitional mode of consciousness (right-handed thinking) and a receptive intuitive mode of consciousness (left-handed thinking). The active intellectual-volitional mode of consciousness has to do with the world of speech, of logic, of reason, of planning, of decision making, and of doing. The receptive intuitive mode of consciousness pertains to the world of symbol, of myth and story, of art and music, of affectivity and emotion, of the imagination. Both modes of consciousness are necessary for us to function as persons in the world. One thinks of talented artists, for example, endowed with rich intuitive gifts yet unable to organize their lives. The church also calls upon both modes of consciousness. The church needs an active intellectual-volitional consciousness in order to pursue its mission in the world to promote the peace and justice of the Kingdom of God. But the church also appeals to the more receptive intuitive consciousness, which is a fertile field for catechesis and liturgy to cultivate. Andrew Greeley has said we need to recapture Catholic sacramental sensibility. There is a religion of theology (right-handed) and a religion of the experience (left-handed). The religion of theology embraces the creed, the catechism, and the institutional church. The religion of experience relates to image, symbol, story, and the story-telling community. We need both. It is not a question of opting for one or even pitting the two against each other; rather, they both need to be present working together. But it so happens that one mode of consciousness, the receptive intuitive, is severely underdeveloped. And this is the mode of consciousness to which catechesis and liturgy directly appeal when we tell the Christian story and celebrate its meaning.

There is another way of looking at the same thing. Primary process thinking has to do with the lived experience of God, the raw experience of our faith. The most immediate response to this experience is to tell the story, the most spontaneous and basic way of naming the experience. Close on the heels of story-telling comes the rite which celebrates and prolongs the meaning of the experience. Theology happens later, a secondary process thinking which happens when we begin to reflect systematically on the story told and the rite celebrated. A good example is the post-resurrection appearances of the Lord. The first reaction after seeing the risen Christ is to tell the story to the other disciples: "We have seen the Lord; he is risen from the tomb." This story-telling of the basic Gospel kerygma that Jesus Christ is the risen Lord forms the nucleus of the Gospel and is the source of all subsequent theological reflection. The next thing the disciples do is to celebrate the meaning of the resurrection. Of the post-resurrection appearances, three of them have to do with the partaking of food—for example, the "breaking of the bread" in Luke 24, in which many exegetes find a primitive eucharist.

The religious imagination draws us into a very primordial experience of God. The living word of Scripture, the witness of the religious experience of the first Christians as set forth by the inspired authors, when proclaimed enables us to identify our own human experiences as being religious experiences, likewise charged with the grace of God. And the religious imagination also helps us to see that it is the mystery of Christ that we celebrate, that we make present in our worship so that we can enter into the saving mystery and become more a part

41

of it, and thus enter more deeply into communion with the Trinity of Father, Son, and Spirit. God chooses to communicate with us, gives God's self to us through forms of imagination. Sacred Scripture itself consists largely of narrative theology, stories. The Gospels tell the greatest story ever told about the greatest life ever lived. And Jesus' preferred way of teaching is not to impart abstract truths but to tell stories. For example, when he expounds upon divine forgiveness, he does not give us abstract truths but tells the parables of mercy (Luke 15): the lost coin, the lost sheep, the prodigal son—or better, the generous, forgiving father. God also communicates to our imagination through the symbols and rituals of the liturgy. A water bath, an anointing with oil, a festive meal with the elements of bread and wine changed into the Body and Blood of Christ: these are symbols which speak to the heart.

John Henry Newman said that faith begins and grows in the imagination. I would suggest that the common enemy to both storytelling and ritual-making is *literalism*. Literalism in storytelling rationalizes the story to such a degree that we wind up with a kind of biblical fundamentalism flourishing in some quarters today. Literalism in ritual-making so stresses the efficaciousness of the liturgy that the symbolic dimension is lost. Robert Hovda once said that efficiency is the greatest enemy of liturgical renewal. To build on this insight further, one could say that our liturgies do not need to be more effective; they need to be more affective. What catechesis needs is a re-mythologizing, a reinterpreting of the Christian story in images and metaphors for today. Read the works of John Shea who is especially good at this. And what liturgy needs is a kind of "second naiveté," as coined by Paul Ricoeur. Let the imagination rediscover the rich symbolic power of a baptismal bath, an anointing with sacred perfume, or the robust and lavish signs of the eucharistic sacrifice.

To make this as concrete as possible, I would like to make five further applications as to how the religious imagination touches upon the work of catechesis and liturgy.

Liturgical Implementation

In retrospect, we can now recognize some of the well-intentioned mistakes at liturgical renewal after the Second Vatican Council. Not that there is anything seriously wrong with the liturgical revisions themselves; they are generally well done. The problem is with our manner of implementation. We were trying to appeal to the more active intellectual-volitional mode of consciousness, whereas the proper appeal should have been directed to the receptive intuitive consciousness, the domain of the religious imagination. For example, we have encouraged noble simplicity, yet sometimes ended up with a barren coldness devoid of any devotional elements with all the warmth of an airplane hanger! We have discouraged repetition, and yet now realize that it is of the nature of good ritual to be somewhat repetitious. One needs to feel at home with a recurring ritual pattern with which you are familiar. C. S. Lewis once said that the Lord enjoined us to feed his sheep, not to experiment with his rats! What makes good liturgy is a balance between a recurring pattern with which people feel comfortable and a place for flexibility where adaptation can be made to particular needs. Liturgical implementation is but one example where the religious imagination can help.

How Liturgy Teaches

Liturgy is not a teaching tool for didactic instruction. Aidan Kavanagh advises: "Liturgy teaches us as any other ritual does, experientially, non-discursively, richly, ambiguously, elementally." In other words, liturgy plugs into the religious imagination of the receptive intuitive mode of consciousness. We should remember that liturgy celebrates saving events, not themes or ideas. There is no quicker way to violate this principle than to begin: "Our theme for this Sunday's Mass is . . ." Right away we are back in the classroom. The paradigm for liturgy should be a ritual celebration, not a classroom experience. The mystagogical principle implies that we do not have to over-explain everything, but rather celebrate it well. And the best catechesis for anything liturgical is well done, prayerful celebration.

The Giftedness of Salvation

A third way the religious imagination can perk up the marriage between catechesis and liturgy is to recover a sense of the giftedness of salvation, the very gratuity of grace. If the active intellectual-volitional consciousness gravitates toward the prayer of petition and intercession, the more receptive mode can lead to a rediscovery of the very giftedness of life, expressed in the much-neglected prayer of praise and thanksgiving. In this way the eucharistic prayer itself will become more and more a paradigm of all Christian prayer. Christianity is first of all what the Father has done for us through Jesus Christ in the power of the Holy Spirit. This presence and action of the Holy Trinity in our lives evokes in turn a response of grateful acknowledgment. This insight can prove to be an antidote to a Pelagian conception of renewal, as if we can somehow manufacture or produce our own salvation. This can help us recover the very giftedness of life, to see how our whole lives are called to be eucharistic, to be acts of thanksgiving and praise of God. To quote again the words of Saint Paul:

> I repeat, it is owing to his favor that salvation is yours through faith. This is not your own doing, it is God's gift; neither is it a reward for anything you have accomplished, so let no one pride himself on it. We are truly his handiwork, created in Christ Jesus to lead a life of good deeds which God prepared for us in advance. (Eph 2:8–10)

The Role of Art

A fourth application of the religious imagination to catechesis and liturgy would be the role of art. We encounter the transcendent God in a special way in the arts, the enrichment of God's creation. The religious imagination opens the door to poetry, to art, to music, to drama, and to dance. Recently I was conversing with some friends about a parish that has done every-thing right in terms of liturgical implementation. Everything a parish is supposed to do, they do: singing at the proper time, doing the liturgy in the way set forth by the General Instruction and the Order of Mass. The moves are all there, but something is lacking and people are leaving the parish. People may leave parishes for a variety of reasons, not all of them necessarily commendable, but in this case the reason was a lack of liturgical artistry. Everything is there, but art and beauty are missing. Patrick Collins feels that good liturgy requires liturgical artists who can create "mystery moments" in the liturgy that relate to moments of mystery in our lives. The most we can do as unworthy planners preparing the liturgy is to help facilitate a religious experience where the Lord can encounter his people. We do this by designing worship services as beautiful, artistic, and tasteful as they can be. John Shea has said that anyone interested in being a liturgist has to have "it." This "it" is an artist's and poet's ability to reflect for others the significance of their experiences as well as the mystery of God in their lives. Our seminary is located near New York City. I find myself constantly encouraging our students to patronize the arts so close-by, telling ceremony people to see a ballet, music people to go to the opera. There is so much to learn here in terms of what we are doing in worship, in terms of cultivating the reli-gious imagination. Andrew Greeley and Mary Durkin claim that worship is a co-relative key that is going to save the church because it brings together and enriches the experiences of life and faith and does this in an artistic manner. In short, to be a religious experience good worship should also be an aesthetic experience as well.

Religious Affectivity

A fifth application where the religious imagination draws catechesis and liturgy together is through a profound and healthy respect for religious affectivity. Religious affectivity is a special way we experience the holy. A frequent criticism of Catholic Christianity since the Council is that we have lost a sense of mystery, of awe, of wonder and transcendence. My contention is that the root problem is that we have not appealed enough to the religious imagination. Our liturgy should be more evocative, more expressive. We need to recover something of the devotional tradition of church, be this adoration of the Blessed Sacrament, devotion to Mary and the saints, the rosary, stations of the cross, or ethnic customs which are passed down from one generation to another. The recovery of the religious imagination is going to be especially vital for any sacramental religion such as Catholic Christianity which seeks to see Christ in all things and all things in Christ. The thesis of Andrew Greeley and Mary Durkin in their book *How to Save the Catholic Church* provides apt advice for catechists and liturgists.

> The Catholic religious experience is sacramental: it encounters God in the events, objects, and persons of every day. The Catholic imagination is analogical: it pictures God as being similar to these events, objects, and persons. The Catholic religious story is cosmic: it believes in happy endings in which grace routs both evil and injustice. The Catholic religious community is organic: it is based on a dense network of local relationships that constitute the matrix of everyday life.[4]

Speaking of happy endings, we have seen how the sometimes estranged marriage partners of catechesis and liturgy have been reconciled through a rediscovery of the connecting bond of evangelization leading to conversion as disclosed by the RCIA and its pastoral application to Christian formation. We have also looked at the religious imagination as an area where both marriage partners could well concentrate in order to improve their communication, to bring a bit more passion and excitment into their union.

We now return to some final words of advice from Pope John Paul II.

4. Andrew M. Greeley and Mary Greeley Durkin, *How to Save the Catholic Church* (New York: Viking, 1984) xx. Chapter 11 was also especially helpful in writing this chapter.

In any case, catechesis always has reference to the sacraments. On the one hand, the catechesis that prepares for the sacraments is an eminent kind, and every form of catechesis necessarily leads to the sacraments of faith. On the other hand, authentic practice of the sacraments is bound to have a catechetical aspect. In other words, sacramental life is impoverished and very soon turns to hollow ritualism if it is not based on serious knowledge of the meaning of the sacraments, and catechesis becomes intellectualized if it fails to come alive in the sacramental practice.

In other words, there exists a complementarity between catechesis and liturgy. Like marriage partners, they are each unique, they are distinct from one another, and yet they desperately need each other in order to survive and prosper. With mutual understanding and affection they can make their marriage work.

A good way to image marriage is to view the husband and wife not turned inward facing each other, but rather holding hands and facing outward so that their marriage is fruitful and life-giving. So it is with the marriage between catechesis and liturgy. It is not simply a question of self-nurture, the two turned in on themselves. Rather, the union has a goal bigger than themselves, namely the mission of the church in the world, to be a credible sign of Christ's presence until he comes again and God will truly be all in all.

CHAPTER 5

A Bill of Rights: Liturgical Adaptation in America

The selection of beautiful and historic San Antonio as the location for the 1977 North American Academy of Liturgy (NAAL) meeting suggested an overarching conference theme of liturgy and cultural adaptation. This modest paper intends to introduce this topic by developing briefly four theses. First, cultural adaptation is a process as old as Christianity itself. Second, cultural adaptation is where the liturgical renewal is at right now. Third, cultural adaptation demands a multidisciplinary approach. Fourth, the challenge is not merely cultural adaptation, but ritual (liturgical) adaptation.

As Old as Christianity

This assertion is easily documented by a survey of various periods in the church's history. Cultural adaptation was at work from the very beginning in the emergence of Christianity from a movement within Judaism to a consciousness of its own identity and mission to the Gentiles, a struggle depicted in the very pages of the New Testament (Acts 15; Gal 1:11–14). Cul-

49

tural adaptation took place in the encounter with the Roman empire, especially after the peace of Constantine and the advent of Christendom. Liturgical traces are found in the development of the church year, for example, the feast of Christmas assigned to the date of the birthday of the invincible sun (*Natalis Solis Invicti*); liturgical vestures appropriated from the senatorial class; and a language whose "soberness and sense" Edmund Bishop claimed to be the genius of the Roman rite.[1] Cultural adaptation continued during the migration of nations and the ensuing missionary activity. In the Eastern Church Cyril and Methodius translated the Bible and liturgical books into Slavonic. In the Western Church this adaptive process ultimately resulted in a fusion of Roman and Gallican elements; the hybrid origins of the modern Roman rite.

In the modern age cultural adaptation led the Reformation communities to the restoration of the vernacular language as a vehicle for proclaiming God's word, to enriched participation consonant with the general priesthood of believers, and, especially in the Church of England, to liturgical creativity. By contrast, the post-Reformation period of the Roman Communion was marked by an almost complete absence of adaptation, at least as far as officially sanctioned services are concerned. The Tridentine and post-Tridentine revisions ushered in an unfortunate centralization of the Roman rite which was to endure until the recent Vatican Council. A single exception to this uniformity was the *Rituale Romanum* of 1614, which was designed for the missions and which—unlike the Roman missal and pontifical—was not imposed but encouraged for the universal church. This reluctance to adapt crippled the missionary outreach of the Roman Church. For example, the suppression

---

1. An alternative thesis for the choice of 25 December to commemorate the birth of Christ is computation of the nativity from the passion, insofar as the date of the death of Jesus would be taken as the date of his conception. See especially Thomas Talley, *The Origins of the Liturgical Year* (New York: Pueblo Publishing Company, 1986), pp.91–99. On liturgical adaptation altogether, see Anscar Chupungco, *Cultural Adaptation of the Liturgy* (New York: Paulist, 1982).

of adaptation to oriental culture virtually sealed the fate of the Jesuit missionary efforts in India and China. And what often goes unnoticed and unmentioned is the apparent failure of all Christian communities to restore and adapt creatively the adult initiation with catechumentate, which had virtually vanished almost a thousand years earlier, to the new world with its vast unchurched population.

Today cultural adaptation is an especially complex course to chart due to parallel developments which have already happened or are happening simultaneously: one the one hand, a movement from a pre-industrial, agrarian society to an industrial technopolis; on the other hand, a movement from a cultural Christianity by inheritance to a faith Christianity by conscious adult decision. The current difficulty lies in discerning the culture to which we are adapting the message, the mystery and the way of Jesus Christ. To sum up, cultural adaptation is a process as old as Christianity because it is an extension of the incarnational principle. The son of God became man so that men and women might become sons and daughters of God.

The Present Stage of Liturgical Renewal

At this very moment the cultural adaptation of worship is occurring all around us. Instances abound, and the following examples are not meant to be exhaustive. In the Roman Communion the 1963 Constitution *Sacrosanctum Concilium* on Sacred Liturgy provided "Norms for Adapting the Liturgy to the Temperament and Traditions of Peoples" (nos. 37–40). In the revision of the Mass and sacraments this is further elaborated in introductions (*praenotanda*) which indicate adaptations to be made by the national episcopal conferences, the local bishop, or the minister. Since 1969 the Inter-Lutheran Commission on Worship has produced the following services in its Contemporary Worship series: *Hymns* (CW 1), *The Holy Communion* (CW 2), *The Marriage Service* (CW 3), *Hymns for Baptism and Holy Communion* (CW 4), *Services of the Word* (CW 5), *The Church Year: Calendar and Lectionary* (CW 6), *Holy Baptism* (CW 7), *Affirmation of the Baptismal Covenant* (CW 8), *Daily Prayer of the*

Church (CW 9), and *Burial of the Dead* (CW 10).[2] The Episcopal revision began in earnest in 1950, with the publication of the first of the Prayer Book Studies which blossomed forth into the *Services for Trial Use* authorized in 1970, and is reaching full fruition in the *Proposed Book of Common Prayer* of 1970.[3] In its turn the United Methodist Church's Alternate Rituals Project has developed *The Sacrament of the Lord's Supper: An Alternate Text 1972*, and in a particularly productive year of 1976: *A Service of Baptism, Confirmation, and Renewal; Word and Table; Ritual in a New Day.*[4]

Do we have any criteria with which to judge the success of cultural adaptation of the liturgy? Help for articulating contemporary criteria for discernment comes to us from such an unlikely source as Dom Prosper Guéranger. Professor Franklin unearthed four negative criteria with which Abbot Guéranger assessed the neo-Gallican liturgies of the last century.[5] These caveats are: 1) false modernity: any liturgical reform must be in touch with the authentic tradition of the church; 2) individualism: liturgical revision must not be the work of one individual; 3) elitism: neither can such reform be the work of a special group—Guéranger undoubtedly had the Jansenists in mind—for this could lead to an unhealthy subjectivism; 4) nationalism. This fourth caveat makes us pause to ponder some of the inherent problems of American civil religion.

Another source of wisdom would be the Vatican decree *Perfectae caritatis* on the Renewal of Religious Life (no. 2) which distinguishes between renewal and adaptation. "The up-to-date renewal [*renovatio*] of the religious life comprises both a constant return to the sources of the whole of the Christian life and to the primitive inspiration of the institutes, and their ad-

2. This project has seen fruition in the publication of the *Lutheran Book of Worship* (Minneapolis: Augsburg Publishing House, 1979).

3. In 1979 the *Proposed Book* became the official *Book of Common Prayer* for the Episcopal Church.

4. The 1984 General Conference adopted a comprehensive *The Book of Services* (Nashville: United Methodist Publishing House, 1985).

5. R. W. Franklin, "Guéranger and Variety in Unity," *Worship* 51 (1977) 378–399.

aptation [*aptatio*] to the changed conditions of our time."[6] Applied to liturgical reform *renewal* means the recovery of the authentic tradition of the church's worship; *adaptation* means enfleshing and continuing this tradition in a culture of a given people who live and worship now, until that day when we are all caught up in the eternal liturgy of the Lamb before the heavenly throne. Is this not at its core a recovery of true symbolic activity: symbols which are not things but real communicative actions whereby an inward reality is both manifested and brought about in and through its outward expression? If successful, such an insight can render the service of recovering the symbolic activity of all human communication, of ecclesial structures and forms of piety and, not least, sacramental ritual itself.

A Multidisciplinary Approach

Like the study of liturgy itself, cultural adaptation also demands a multidisciplinary treatment. In our own day we can recall a chronological progression in the study of liturgics: from the juridical to the historical to the theological and now to the present emphasis on the behavioral sciences. According to the *juridical* approach, liturgy was a branch of canon law as then practiced. Canon lawyers were the first liturgists and the most important question asked was a rubrical one: "Can you do it?" The *historical* approach—"How was the liturgy celebrated in the past?"—flourished as a result of the important research of such scholars as A. Baumstark, G. Dix, J. A. Jungmann, and Th. Klauser. On the basis of their liberating findings, the study of worship was able to move into a *theological* phase: "What is the meaning of liturgy?" This rediscovery of the *lex orandi, lex credendi* was consummated in the happy remarriage of the long estranged partners of sacramental theology and liturgics, as evidenced in the writings of C. Vagaggini, E. Schillebeeckx, A. Verheul, and E. Kilmartin.

6. Austin Flannery, ed., *Vatican II: The Conciliar and Post Conciliar Documents* (Collegeville: The Liturgical Press, 1975) 612.

The experiential concern of the present interest in behavioral sciences is "How to celebrate the liturgy well." Anthropologists such as Mary Douglas and Victor Turner have demonstrated the intrinsic dynamics of what happens when the human person in community celebrates ritual. From psychology we learn how much of worship, especially nonverbal symbols, sinks roots into the depths of the unconscious mind. Sociologists tell us about the people for whom we are adapting the liturgy. For example, the recent survey on the impact of liturgical renewal among Roman Catholics, while recording a basically positive response to liturgical change, did observe two negative reactions: one is the introduction of special eucharistic ministers and the other, the elimination of popular devotions and benediction.[7] Upon reflection, perhaps the former could have been obviated by the prior introduction of communion in the hand, whereas the latter distress once again points out the need for bridges between prayer alone and liturgical prayer, be these popular devotions, liturgies of the word or paraliturgies, shared prayer, or the liturgy of the hours.

In this multidisciplinary enterprise which characterizes both the study of liturgics and the process of cultural adaptation, the role of the NAAL becomes more sharply defined. The Academy has adopted an integrated, multidisciplinary approach which brings together in sharing collaboration canon lawyers, historians, theologians, behavioral scientists, artists and architects, musicians and dancers. The NAAL insists that the science of liturgics and related disciplines are to be taken seriously. And it pursues this goal in the only way possible, as an ecumenical endeavor.

Not Merely Cultural but Ritual-Liturgical Adaptation

The cultural adaptation of worship must not neglect the role of liturgy as Christian religious ritual. Liturgical reform in

7. William C. McCready, *Changing Attitudes of American Catholics Toward the Liturgy: A National Survey 1974* (Chicago: National Opinion Research Center, 1975).

America has been variously described as marked by amateurism, pragmatism, and consumerism. Perhaps at the heart of the matter is the question of whether we even know how to celebrate ritual. Here are some disturbing symptoms of this malaise of our being unable to get inside the experience of worship. 1) The rapid, almost thoughtless pace of revision, as if overnight we could overhaul ritual patterns—the most conservative feature of any group or religion—and expect people to feel at home with them. 2) The excessive wordiness and didactism of worship. The paradigm for liturgy has become no longer the ritual event but the classroom. Together with textual revision must go a corresponding concentration on such non-verbal features as baptism by immersion and a eucharist with real bread and wine. 3) An uneasiness with formality and repetition. Margaret Mead well describes the situation: "Contemporary American celebrations suffer from our objection to anything we can classify as ritualistic, repetitive or even familiar."[8] 4) Music and art considered as decorative features, rather than intrinsic to a celebration which demands full human and artistic expression. 5) The overuse of the Mass as a ritual form for every occasion: a tendency endemic to Roman Catholic circles. 6) The incapacity to celebrate a feast. We so overanticipate Christmas in the season of Advent that we are exhausted and resourceless by 25 December. We have yet to discover what the season of Easter is all about: the fifty-day continuous celebration of the Lord Jesus' death and resurrection. Our annual paschal observance seems to come to a grinding halt on Easter Sunday. For many, liturgical services continue to be individual, devotional exercises, rather than the public ritual prayer of the faith community of the church.

Some years ago an essay in *Time* magazine vividly depicted the American bill of rites:

The gift of ritual is not exactly prospering in the 20th century; secularity, urbanism, technology—all contrive to separate mod-

8. Margaret Mead, *Twentieth Century Faith: Hope and Survival.* Religious Perspectives, vol. 25 (New York: Harper & Row, 1972) 124.

ern man from the kind of community that encourages, even
demands, a sense of ceremony. But is this the best that American can do for a bill of rites? Other people's rituals tend to
release them—as they should. Rituals are society's unwritten
permission for civilized man to express primtive emotions: fear,
sexuality, grief. Other people's rituals invite them to be more
human in public—more themselves—than they dare to be in
private. Greek Zorbas whirl like fertility gods, Irishmen keen at
their friends' funerals or even the funerals of strangers. Americans smile their Fixed Smile: the smile that tries to hide the face
of American Gothic and only betrays it. The smile that says, "I
cannot be myself in public."[9]

If this predicament in the nonreligious sphere rings true, it is
small wonder that we have problems ritualizing the experience
of Jesus' dying and rising and our participation in this saving
mystery.

Where is hope for the future? We must begin where we are,
with what we have. One avenue for the future recovery of
ritual would be to reexamine and to treasure our cultural diversity and ethnicity.

We could begin to appreciate ethnic customs supportive of
worship. For example, an Italian meal is a ritual event which
reminds us that the sharing of food is not a hasty occasion for
nourishment, but a sharing of yourself with others. The
eucharistic implications are obvious. Or again, the Polish
oplatek: bread broken and shared among the family members
at Christmas as they beg mutual forgiveness for any hurt or
offense they may have caused during the year. This manner
of interpersonal reconciliation could be a head start to celebrating reconciliation liturgies in the church.

We must begin to study the worship experiences of native
Americans, black Americans, Mexican Americans. Native
Americans demonstrate how a closeness to nature, a sense of
wonder, is a precondition for worship. Black Americans know
that we worship not just with our head; rather we praise the

9. Melvin Maddocks, "Rituals—The Revolt Against the Fixed Smile," *Time*
(12 October 1970) 42.

Father through the Son in the Holy Spirit with the whole person: memory, imagination, body, feeling, and, above all, the heart. And if our Academy is called the North American Academy of Liturgy and our chosen topic is liturgical adaptation in America, our concern must embrace all North Americans, including the Mexican American experience. It is ironic that the people most disenfranchised from the American dream may be the ones who can best help us recover our bill of rites.

Sundays
and
Weekdays

Celebrating Sunday Liturgy: Present and Future

CHAPTER 6

Several years ago an issue on the ballot in many states was the Sunday closing law. The arguments heard pro and con differed from place to place, according to the wording of the referendum, but the specific issue of business as usual seven days a week raised the broader issue of Sunday observance. Why is Sunday different from any other day? Why rest on Sunday? Why attend Mass?

The underlying assumption of these pages is that if the celebration of Sunday liturgy had greater meaning for Catholics, these questions would not arise—or at least, the answer to them might be different. Accordingly, we shall briefly examine the meaning of the Sunday eucharistic assembly in the tradition of the church; then pose six pastoral questions for the present; and finally, conclude with some practical suggestions for the future. Hopefully, a better understanding of the significance of Sunday will help restore its observance to the place it once had in Christian culture.

The Sunday Eucharistic Assembly

To be a Christian means to be a member of the Christian assembly, the church (*ekklesia*), as realized in the local community of the parish. God calls us by our first name, but saves us as a people. The vocation to be a Christian always includes other people. From start to finish the Christian religion is profoundly communal.

The Christian assembly gathers together to celebrate the eucharist, the Lord's Supper, the Mass, in order to be true to our identity. We remember Jesus as he asked to be remembered on the night before he died (1 Cor 11:25). We celebrate the paschal mystery of the new covenant which has formed us into a people.

The community assembles on Sunday. Why Sunday and not Tuesday or Friday? Sunday is the original Christian feast day, the "weekly" Easter.[1] Sunday is the day of Jesus' resurrection from the dead (Mt 28:1; Mk 16:9; Lk 24:1; Jn 20:1). Sunday is the day he appeared to his own, when he reunited his scattered disciples and, as it were, "re-instituted" the eucharist (Lk 24:35). Sunday is thus the "day of the Lord": the memorial of his resurrection on the first day of the week, the beginning of a new creation.[2] It is also an anticipation of his future coming, the consummation of all time and history on the eighth day of the week. And on Sundays Christians assemble here and now to be formed more completely into church through word, sacrament, and sharing love.

The need to celebrate "the Lord's day" is the basis for all

1. On the tradition of the Christian Sunday, see Willy Rordorf, *Sunday: The History of the Day of Rest and Worship in the Earliest Centuries of the Christian Church* (Philadelphia: Westminster Press, 1968); Adolf Adam, *The Liturgical Year* (New York: Pueblo Publishing Company, 1981) 35–56; A. G. Martimort, ed., *The Church at Prayer*. Vol. 4: *The Liturgy and Time* (Collegeville: The Liturgical Press, 1986) 9–29.

2. The "day of the Lord," *dominicus dies* (Latin languages: *dimanche, domenica, domingo*) is a phrase which first occurs in Rev 1:10 and by the fifth century had supplanted the *dies solis* (Germanic languages: Sunday, *Sonntag*) in the legal nomenclature of the days of the week.

other secondary meanings assigned to Sunday. Rooted in the most ancient tradition of the church (1 Cor 16:2; Acts 20:6–12), the notion of Sunday eucharistic assembly is grounded more deeply than the Code of Canon Law.[3] It transcends any juridical obligation narrowly and individualistically conceived. It was another of the many achievements of the Second Vatican Council to recover the principle, deeply embedded in the theology of Saint Paul, that the universal church, manifested in the local community, is *realized* in the eucharistic celebration of this local assembly (*ekklesia*).[4] This insight is at the heart of the present reform of the church.

The Sunday eucharistic assembly also has priority over the motif of *Sabbath rest*. The abstention from servile work was a practice introduced only in the fourth century after the peace of Constantine. Whatever the religious significance of Sabbath rest in the law of the Old Covenant, its immediate purpose in the Christian community was to guarantee the working class (*servi*) an opportunity of worship and catechetical instruction. In a contemporary culture, so bent on production, consumerism, and pragmatism, however, Sunday rest has taken on new significance. We have a great need for simply being, not always doing. There is a close affinity between wonder and worship, play and prayer. Gerard Sloyan puts it well when he asserts that a perennial value of Sunday is "being made whole in the company of others."[5]

The Sunday eucharistic assembly has a significance which should not be obscured because of sheer convenience of scheduling or attendance. This is a danger, for example, when mistaken reasons are offered to explain why the Sunday Mass may

3. The new Code of Canon Law properly highlights Sunday as the primordial holyday, "the foremost holyday of obligation in the universal Church" (canon 1246).

4. See Constitution on the Church, no. 26.

5. Gerard S. Sloyan, "Sunday—Being Made Whole in the Company of Others," *Liturgy* 20 (April 1975) 108–113. Both this entire issue as well as volume 20 (December 1975), which contains the proceedings of the Thirty-First North American Liturgical Week, are devoted to a consideration of Sunday.

be anticipated on Saturday evening. It is not a question of Mass on any day during the week, or merely making it easier to fulfill an obligation. Rather, the sound pastoral and historical reasons why a portion of the assembly may (and does) begin its Sunday celebration on Saturday evening, need to be emphasized.

Pastoral Questions for the Present

If the significance of the Sunday eucharistic assembly is to be experienced and properly understood, we must pay careful attention to the quality of parish life as expressed in the Sunday liturgy. Some hard questions must be asked about present practice. I suggest beginning with questions which, while they focus on pastoral practice, touch on deeper, underlying issues.[6]

How much does each member feel he/she belongs? Whenever we celebrate a ritual of any kind, we are spelling out in word and symbol the meaning of some experience we are having. For example, a birthday party ritualizes the significance of another year of life for a person we hold dear. The various bicentennial celebrations that took place in 1986 were an attempt—sporadically successful—to spell out the meaning of two hundred years existence as a nation. As a result of any ritual celebration, the experience is both expressed and also deepened, prolonged, intensified.

What, then, is the experience we ritualize in Sunday Mass? Is it nothing less than everything it means to be church. We come together both to express and to deepen this identity as church which comes about from our weekly celebration of the paschal mystery. And so to ask how much does each member feel he/she belongs is the same thing as to ask what does it mean to be church?

Does the assembly perform a pastoral service, initiating and strengthening the faith of its members? One of the most neglected insights of Vatican II's liturgical reform is found in the Constitution on the Sacred Liturgy:

6. These questions are adapted from Casiano Floristán, "The Assembly and Its Pastoral Implications," *Concilium* 12, 1966, 40–43.

> The sacred liturgy does not exhaust the entire activity of the church. Before men can come to liturgy they must be called to faith and to conversion. (no. 9)

What is really at stake is the process of evangelization and conversion as carried out in parochial life. Here the Rite of Christian Initiation of Adults represents an important break-through. The initiation of adults, of mature candidates capable of a conscious faith commitment, is perceived as theologically normative. The initiation of children, in particular, infant baptism, is a pastoral application of the meaning of adult initiation whereby the children are initiated into the faith of the church as professed by their parents. For both adults and children alike, Christian initiation always involves a process of coming to faith and conversion in the Christian church. Whether the catechumenate for adults or the Christian education of children (a type of post-baptismal catechumenate), the initiation process is always multi-dimensional: doctrinal, liturgical, apostolic, and communal. This initiation experience is sacramentalized in baptism, confirmation, and eucharist, always the sacraments of Christian initiation at whatever age they are celebrated.

The church exists not only to bring people to faith and conversion in Christ but also to sustain and nourish the initial faith of those already converted. Some of the ways the local parish can sustain and nourish the faith of its parishioners would be through a well-coordinated season of Lent-Easter, a prayerful celebration of the revised Rite of Penance, a vibrant adult education program, and a Sunday eucharist which is christocentric both in liturgical celebration and homiletic proclamation.

What relationships does the assembly have beyond itself? In regard to the diocesan assembly and larger church, does the parish feel part of a wider whole or is it enmeshed in parochialism? Is there an ecumenical interest and concern for other Christian communions and for our Jewish brothers and sisters? What relationship does the assembly have to the broader human community: a sense of mission and ministry as a sign and instrument of the Kingdom of God at work in the world?

How diversified and full is the ministerial expression of the assembly?

The *priest* (presbyter). His liturgical presidency of leadership at prayer is the sacramental expression of his charge at ordination to build up the local faith community through a leadership that encourages and activates the charisms and ministries of the entire parish.

The *deacon*. Although the permanent deacon is a preeminent minister of charity, he functions liturgically as an intermediary (e.g., calls to prayer, petitions, dismissal) and the ideal master of ceremonies.

The *special ministers of the eucharist* are needed to facilitate communion, especially under both kinds on Sundays, as well as to minister to the sick and elderly of the parish or hospital. It is appropriate that the special ministers be drawn from the parish for they represent the community administering to its own.

Readers or lectors must consistently work at the quality of their proclamation, so as to wean people away from an obsessive dependence upon missalettes.

Ministers of music. The choir, instrumentalists, and especially leaders of song are needed more than ever, both for folk and for more traditional church music. Every effort must be made to integrate the hymns with the celebration so to focus the attention of the assembly on what they are about.

Servers should be well versed in the meaning of the Mass so as to participate more fully. And why not altar girls?

Ushers. Some parishes have inaugurated the practice of host families, where entire families—parents and children—take turns greeting old parishioners and welcoming new ones.

Are all these ministers well-trained and well-prepared, not only in terms of technical skills such as presidency, proclamation, or musicianship, but also insofar as they are imbued with a sense of the spirituality of the ministry they exercise in the service of their brothers and sisters? Are the ministers representative of the makeup of the parish: different ethnic, racial, and economic groups, varying ages from young to elderly; both sexes? Is there some collaborative planning of the Sunday liturgy?

How suitable is the place of worship? The current trend in ecclesial art and architecture is a movement away from a fascination with objects in favor of a people-oriented liturgy. Recall that the term "church" was first predicated of the faith community, and only later and secondarily of the place where the community assembled for worship.

As related to the liturgical renewal, one can discern three steps. First came the revision of liturgical books, now virtually completed. The second stage—where we are right now—is how to celebrate these revised rites in a prayerful communal manner. The third stage which evolves from this and will occupy us considerably more in the future is the critical need for the proper environment for a prayerful communal celebration of these revised rites. One good example of this is the spatial setting demanded for the communal celebration of the revised Order of Mass, whereby the participants are gathered more closely around the table of the Lord. Another example is the environment for worship presupposed by the revised Rite of Penance: neither a darkened confessional, nor a private counseling chamber, but a spatial area in the church which makes for a more personalized encounter with the forgiving Christ in his reconciling church.

How active is the participation of each member of the assembly? "Full, conscious, and active participation" remains the primary aim of liturgical renewal.[7] The term "conscious" includes the inward awareness and appropriation of both the experience celebrated and the ritual of celebration. It presumes catechesis on the revised rites as they are implemented—and the most enduring and thorough catechesis is a well-done reverent celebration.

What is to be done in particular with the planning of the Sunday liturgy? Liturgy is Christian religious ritual. As all ritual, there is a recurring pattern and a place for flexibility. For example, there is a basic pattern in the new Order of Mass which recurs: this is healthy and good, for it is of the nature of ritual to be somewhat formal and repetitive. The place for flexibility in the revised Mass is found in the multiple options (mu-

7. Constitution on the Sacred Liturgy, no. 14.

sic, penitential rite, intercessions, prayers, etc.) which allow for adaptations to the local assembly.

What about theme Masses? There is usually some discernible motif(s) suggested by the season or scripture readings, which should be the basis for selecting the various options and should find its greatest unfolding in the homily. But beware of an overly thematic concentration. Consider, for example, the number of theme Sundays we celebrate—all of them ostensibly for a good cause—from Right to Life to the Propagation of Faith. As one beleagured priest exclaimed, "Every Sunday has a name!"

Ritual is an art form, and it is of the essence of art to be subtle. Furthermore, in our liturgy we do not celebrate ideas, but rather the saving mystery of Jesus Christ. The paradigm for liturgical celebration is not the classroom, but the ritual event. Liturgy is first and foremost prayer, the public prayer of the church, and not a teaching tool. It teaches as all ritual teaches: indirectly, nondiscursively, subliminally.

The greatest single problem with our celebration of liturgy today is the wordiness of worship, the excessive didacticism which almost unnoticed creeps into our intercessory prayers and even leaves its imprint on such iconographic forms as banners! Or again, a child returning home after Sunday Mass was polled by its parents regarding the homily, to which the child retorted: "Which one?"

We must find ways to stem this rampant tide of words. For one thing, we need to articulate these words better, be they words of proclamation or words of prayer: celebrants who mean what they say when they pray the eucharistic prayer, intercessions that can be remembered, Glorias and Creeds which are something more than going through the motions. Comments, when employed, should truly say something, leading people more into the celebration of the mystery of Christ, not driving them away. We also need to sing more words, especially those parts of the Mass that cry out for musical expression, such as the responsorial psalm and the eucharistic acclamations. We need more responsorial and antiphonal singing, not just a steady diet of metric hymns. And at the same time we could also do with fewer words and more time for silence and prayerful reflection.

We have also not yet begun to exploit the non-verbal features of liturgical celebration. Rather than remaining content with a sacramental minimalism and vocal maximalism, we should develop the non-verbal symbols which reach so deeply into the unconscious of the human personality of worship. Here are some of the areas of non-verbal communication and participation which could use improvement.

Eucharistic meal with bread and wine. The elements for communion should be consecrated at the same Mass, not taken from the tabernacle. The bread should resemble bread: why do we perpetuate wafer hosts? Maybe this is one reason why the fraction rite, one of the four principal actions of the Mass (take, bless, *break*, share), to be accompanied by the sung Lamb of God, is so woefully neglected. Communion under two kinds should be an option extended above all other times at the Sunday eucharistic assembly.

Bodily movement. Why do we stand, kneel, sit, bow, or genuflect? Perhaps the other participants at worship might also imitate the *orantes* gesture of the extended hands of the celebrant, for example, at the Lord's Prayer. We could use more processions of the people, not just the ministers, as well as drama, mime, and liturgical dance.

Other symbols. Water: the baptismal/holy water font and updated asperges or sprinkling are all important baptismal reminders. Fire/light appeals to the sense of sight, as does incense to the sense of smell.

Participation aids. A better job could be done with missalettes and bulletins, which often display an utter absence of art and professionalism.

Practical Suggestions for the Future

Having restated the tradition of Sunday as the day for the Sunday eucharistic assembly and having reviewed the pastoral implications of this, we now close with practical suggestions for the future. A parish liturgy team could begin to revitalize its

Sunday liturgy by considering some of the following suggestions.

1. Be familiar with the liturgy documents, especially the excellent pastoral-theological introductions to the new rites, for example, the General Instruction to the new Order of Mass which is reprinted in every sacramentary as well as published separately.[8] These rites represent the authentic liturgical tradition of the church.

2. Embark on a consciousness-raising of other ways that American people ritualize experiences, both nonreligious and religious, for example, bicentennial celebrations, the pervasive influence of American civil religion, ethnic customs, the Protestant tradition.

3. Give attention to ministries already existing or yet to be implemented. Perhaps a ministerial day meeting with the respective ministers might be in order to show the appreciation of the parish and to provide technical and motivational support.

4. Evaluate all liturgical services—not just the eucharist. Review the scheduling: for example, are there more Masses than needed? Develop criteria for evaluation and apply them. Maybe a parish questionnaire would be helpful. Video-taping a Sunday liturgy would be ideal.

5. Provide feedback on preaching in a positive, constructive way. Suggest ideas for future homilies, especially topics seldom touched upon.

6. Examine the liturgical space for celebration. It is usually not just a question of renovating a sanctuary, but of providing a proper worship environment for all the participants so that the new liturgy can really work.

7. Consider the overall prayer life of the parish. There is a pressing need to cultivate sound habits of personal prayer alone, as well as to provide bridges to liturgical prayer. Catholic popular devotions, paraliturgies, shared prayer, and now espe-

8. Every member of a parish liturgy team should study *The Liturgy Documents* rev. and ed. by Mary Ann Simcoe (Chicago: Liturgy Training Publications, 1985).

cially the revised communal format for the Liturgy of the Hours (Divine Office) are some of the ways.

We praise the Father for the progress made in the liturgical reform. We continue to seek the wisdom of his Holy Spirit to inspire our celebration of Jesus' dying and rising. We still have to learn how to get more inside of the lived, participated experience of Christian religious ritual which we call liturgy. And the renewal of the Sunday liturgy will always remain as much an ecclesial concern as a liturgical one: Sunday Mass is the assembly of the local Christian community for worship.

When you are teaching, command and exhort the people to be faithful to the assembly of the church. Let them not fail to attend, but let them gather faithfully together. Let no one deprive the Church by staying away; if they do, they deprive the body of Christ of one of its members! For you must not think only of others but of yourself as well, when you hear the words that our Lord spoke: "Who does not gather with me, scatters" (Mt 12:30). Since you are the members of Christ, you must not scatter yourselves outside the Church by failing to assemble there. For we have Christ for our Head, as he himself promised and announced, so that "You have become shareres with us." Do not, then, make light of your own selves, do not deprive our Saviour of his members, do not rend, do not scatter his Body.[9]

9. *Didascalia* chapter 13 (third century, Syriac). Translation from Lucien Deiss, *Springtime of the Liturgy* (Collegeville: The Liturgical Press, 1979) 176–177.

CHAPTER 7

Is It Worship? Evaluating the Sunday Liturgy

Very often in teaching a course in liturgy I will begin by asking the students to describe a nonreligious celebration in which they participated that left a lasting impression. They have come up with all sorts of diverse celebrations: the Olympics, a baseball or football game, the inauguration of a president, a graduation ceremony, a birthday party, a testimonial dinner, and so on. Usually a particular event is chosen because it was either a very positive experience or else a very negative one. The students are then asked to indicate why they feel a given ritual was so successful or conversely so disastrous. The point of this project is to enable the students to sharpen their own powers of discernment and to develop sound value judgments that can be applied *mutatis mutandis* to religious ritual or liturgy.

The renewal of the church has entered a stage of accountability. It is time to search out criteria by which to evaluate our worship. The following seven criteria are suggested primarily for the eucharistic worship of the Sunday assembly, but there is no reason why they would not apply equally well to any communal or festive celebration of a sacrament, the Liturgy of the Hours, or whatever. While the criteria are intended first of all for parish communities, they can also be adapted for any community of Christians gathered together for worship.

Is it WORSHIP?

Wholeness—is the worship related to the total life of the parish faith community?

Organized—is it planned and prepared?

Ritual—are there good signs and symbols?

Shared—is there participation?

Harmonious balance of components that make up the total experience?

Integrity of form, especially in the liturgical environment and various parts of Mass?

Prayerful? Last, but certainly not least, this is the most important criterion.

Wholeness in Relation to Total Parish Life

Writing from a theological perspective on the persistence of religion, David Power has persuasively articulated the conditions for a Christian religion that mediates faith. It must treat of ultimate realities: "life and death, evil, sin, personal worth and community belonging, or reconciliation and brotherhood among men."[1] There must be a personal dimension: an interiorization process, which is at the heart of church renewal today. This personal element should further blossom forth into a witness of life, a sense of mission expressed in social concern and action. There is also a necessary institutional dimension at

1. David Power, "A Theological Perspective on the Persistence of Religion," *Concilium*, New Series, 1/9, 91–105.

the service of the total community. Historical consciousness, too, is needed in a revealed religion with a rich tradition that reaches back into our Jewish roots. Systematic or theological reflection on the experience of faith is also vital. Finally there is a poetic and symbolic expression in which Power would locate the liturgical life of a community of faith.

What I wish to stress here is that, while the liturgy is the church's greatest self-expression and actualization, it is not everything the church does. Many people have been frustrated by the apparent failure of the revised liturgy to create the perfect Christian community. Perhaps their expectations of liturgy as the "source and summit of Christian life" were unrealistic. More likely, they may have considered liturgy in a kind of vacuum apart from the many other dimensions that make up a vibrant Christian community. The problem is that the liturgy is a constant: it is always celebrated week-in, week-out.

When the ultimate realities of life are obscured in the church's proclamation, when there is little or no personal appropriation of social witness, when there is either an absence or a preponderance of institution, when historical consciousness or theological reflection are lacking, then the liturgy must bear the brunt of this impoverishment, which gradually becomes an intolerable burden. In other words, many problems that seem to be liturgical have an extra-liturgical source. The parish will be truly alive only when all the components that make up church are working together. A sense of wholeness in relation to the total life of the parish community is the first criterion by which one may judge an effective liturgy.

Organized

Is the service well-planned and prepared or has it been hastily put together on the spot? The revised liturgy with its many options demands some prior planning and coordination. Moreover, it requires some collaborative preparation. If the norm for Mass is a communal celebration of the Sunday assembly of God's people, then people should be represented and involved at all the steps along the way.

In planning the celebration, the priest should consider the spiritual good of the assembly rather than his own desires. The choice of texts is to be made in consultation with the ministers and others who have a function in the celebration, including the faithful, for the parts which belong to them.[2]

Ideally, a planning meeting begins with and sustains a prayerful atmosphere. At the start the opening prayer of the Sunday Mass may be read. The planning group can then reflectively share and meditate upon the Scripture assigned for the Sunday. Sermon material and musical selections will gradually suggest themselves. Any thematic coherence that results should flow from the proclaimed word and the liturgical season. Avoid over-thematization: liturgy is not a classroom lecture but a ritual event. Moreover, ritual worship is a complex art form; it is of the nature of art to be subtle and poetic. We might also recall that liturgical organization is not exhausted on the drawing boards by filling in the textual options on a planning sheet. It can be useful to have the ministers "walk through" the rite from time to time. Is the liturgical choreography smooth? More specifically, what about the manner of entrance of ministers and their reverence of the altar? Is the reader at home with the microphone? What does the procession of gifts look like? The sharing of communion? Do the ministers of the celebration consult with one another beforehand and agree about who will do what and when? If we regularly conduct wedding rehearsals before the marriage liturgy, why not also arrange for an occasional practice with the ministers of Sunday worship?

Ritual

Is the liturgy sensual, evocative, affective, and moving? Is it a humanly attractive religious experience? In other words, it is good religious ritual? Sometimes people are startled by the remarks: "I enjoyed Mass. It felt good." Maybe we have yet to

2. General Instruction of the Roman Missal, no. 313. See also no. 73.

completely overcome a Jansenist-tainted approach to spirituality and asceticism that confuses fasting and feasting. And when comments about the liturgy are forthcoming, they usually relate to the quality of the homily: one more instance of a misconception of liturgy as a kind of head trip or cerebral exercise. We must learn to outgrow an ingrained reluctance to accept the fact that liturgy is a ritual activity. As John Gallen has tirelessly pointed out, liturgy is spelling out in word and action the meaning of a given experience—for Christians the paschal mystery in which we are invited to share—in a way that both expresses the experience and deepens or prolongs it. Religious ritual or liturgy is, furthermore, an enterprise involving the whole person in community: heart, mind, memory, imagination, emotions, the unconscious, the body, masculinity and femininity.

Here are some practical solutions to help overcome the excessive wordiness of worship and to recover something of its ritual content:

1. Mean what you say with the words you do use. Words are important! We need presiding celebrants who pray with deliberateness and conviction, especially the eucharistic prayer. Readers could profit from experiencing Alec McCowen's solo narration of Saint Mark's Gospel as an example of how effective and compelling story-telling can be. Congregations should speak up and out of this dialogue or participatory prayer that makes up our worship.

2. Cultivate periods of sacred silence as an opportunity for the worshipers to interiorize spiritually and psychologically what they are doing and saying together. "Let us pray" is not a cue for the server to come over with the sacramentary; it is a serious call to reflective prayer. Silence is particularly helpful after communion inasmuch as the revised Mass comes to a rather hasty conclusion.

3. Sing more of the words, especially those parts that should be sung, but avoid the four-hymn syndrome. The responsorial psalm is meant to be sung. The Alleluia may be omitted—and should be—when not sung. The acclamations of the eucharistic prayer (Holy, Holy, Holy Lord, memorial acclamation, Amen)

when sung enable us to recover the great prayer of thanksgiving as one which the entire community can claim as its own according to different roles and ministries. Hymns should be interesting to sing with words that make sense.

4. Pay attention to nonverbal symbols. Sacraments are not things, for example, water, oil, bread and wine. They are symbolic actions: a bath with water, a liberal anointing with oil, a eucharistic meal with real bread and wine. Encourage other forms of nonverbal participation: have the congregation stand during the eucharistic prayer, pray the Lord's Prayer with hands extended, and be involved more often in procession or even dance.

Shared

This is another way of expressing the primary aim of liturgical reform, the "full, conscious and active participation" of the faithful. It does not necesssarily refer first of all to the volume of sound or the liveliness of movement. Rather, it means that people know why they are there and what is happening, so that they can both inwardly and outwardly enter into the celebration. Are they happy to be there? Is there a sense of oneness? Do the people "own" their worship: have they appropriated it interiorly and adapted it to their own needs.

In this regard, the expanded sense of ministries is a development to be welcomed: deacons, readers, acolytes or eucharistic ministers, musicians, ushers or ministers of hospitality. They should be competent, well-prepared, motivated, and representative of the different ages, backgrounds, and sexes of the parishioners. Many parishes have found great benefit in periodically calling together the various ministers for an updating session and self-reflection on their respective ministries. The aim of these expanded ministries is far from a kind of clericalism once removed; it is an attempt to contextualize ministry within the people of God. Ministry is precisely service of the people of God, and the ministers should function so as to draw attention not to themselves but rather to the mystery of Christ we celebrate together. The surest way to evaluate the effectiveness of the individual ministries—those of priests and bishops included—is to discern how well they have activated the basic ministry of all the baptized and made others feel more a part of the church.

When we ask if the liturgy is shared, we are really talking about the integrity of the eucharist as the sacrament of the unity of the church. Mary Collins has suggested evaluating the communion rite to see what model of the church is operative in it. We might use some of Victor Turner's categories to ask *exegetically* whether people have grasped the meaning of communion as union with Christ and with each other, the whole body of Christ which is the church. Look for the care with which the sign of peace is exchanged and the unitive symbolism of the much-neglected fraction rite during the Lamb of God. *Operationally*, who is doing what as regards the manner of communion: eucharistic bread that resembles bread, communion with the cup, use of ministers? *Positionally*, what is the use of the total spatial environment: are people simply lining up for communion, or is it a procession to receive the sacrament of the Lord's body and blood, which binds us together and makes us church?

Harmonious Balance

Does the celebration flow? Does it hang together? Obviously not all the parts of the Mass are of equal importance. For example, the most important features of the introductory or gathering rites, a kind a vestibule leading to word and eucharist, are the entrance song, greeting, and opening prayer. Or again, the eucharistic prayer is vastly more important than the preparation of the gifts and should be celebrated as such. Fr. Elmer Pfeil has constructed a helpful diagram illustrating the inner rhythm of the Mass.[3] It is similar to the "proclamation/response cadence chart" found in the *Modern Liturgy Handbook*.[4]

3. *Gemshorn* 16:3.
4. John Mossi, ed., *Modern Liturgy Handbook* (Ramsey, NJ: Paulist Press, 1976).

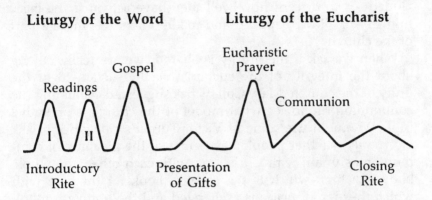

We might further explore whether there is a harmonious balance between action and contemplation in worship; between repetition (continuity) and flexibility (discontinuity); between corporate expression and individual needs, as much as these can be provided for in the public worship of the church. We are just beginning to fathom the psychological factors of worship, which with its archetypal symbols sinks its taproots deeply into the unconscious mind. Much of the needed harmonious balance and rhythm can be achieved through the skillful use of music and nonverbal symbols, which can exercise a cohesive effect on the many words of worship.

Integrity of Form

During a practicum for future presiding celebrants I quizzed one of the participants about his rather flat and unexpressive gestures. "Why in the first place do you even raise your hands in prayer?" I asked. When he replied that it was in the rubrics, I challenged him to realize that the extended hands of the priest have to be more than hands aimlessly flagging in the air. There are, for instance, gestures of greeting, gestures of petition addrsssed to the Father in a presidential prayer, and an epicletic gesture over the gifts. Form follows function. There is a reason why things are the way they are. This underlying reason can generally be found in the excellent introductions to the revised rites and should be translated into action.

Form follows function. The altar is the table of the Lord, not a dumping ground for missalettes, cards, intercessions, and the like—"litter-gy," as one person has put it. There should be nothing placed on the altar until the preparation of gifts. One lectern or ambo with one lectionary, not a missalette, is the proper spatial environment for the proclamation of the word. The presidential chair should be visible but not imposing, in keeping with the presiding celebrant's responsibility of leadership in liturgical prayer. We might also give attention to the aesthetic attractiveness and class of parish bulletins and whatever participation aids are provided.

Form follows function. Sunday Mass is the weekly assembly of God's people to celebrate the eucharist on the Day of the Lord, the little Easter in the church week. As regards scheduling, is there enough time between Masses to facilitate this coming together of the local church? Are there more Masses than needed, fostering the impression that our Sunday liturgy is more a matter of personal convenience than worship together.

The Bishops' Committee on the Liturgy has some fine things to say about the integrity of liturgical symbols, deploring both a tendency to duplicate them with a resulting diminution, and also a tendency to make up for weak primary symbols with secondary ones.[5] I was once approached about the propriety of flowers in the procession of gifts at a graduation Mass. My only concern was not to neglect the primary symbols of bread and cup, for it is these and not the flowers that we eat and drink at communion!

Form follows function. Two places for textual creativity where this especially applies are the penitential rite, Form C, and the general intercessions. One could argue against the appropriateness of the penitential rite at the beginning of Mass. It is psychologically abrupt. Theologically it is perhaps unsound since conversion should follow, not precede, the proclamation of the word. Liturgically it is misleading, for the entire

5. "Environment and Art in Catholic Worship" no. 86.

eucharist is a sacrifice of reconciliation; and pastorally it is not necessary at every Mass. Nonetheless, it is there. What are we to do with it? The most penitential of penitential rites is Form A, the *Confiteor*, particularly fitting for Lent. As the models in the sacramentary show, Form C, the least penitential, is not meant to be a moralistic examination of conscience as such ("For the times that we . . ."), but is an attractive way of integrating the "Lord have mercy" with invocations of praise and thanksgiving addressed to Christ. These may be easily drawn from the readings, especially the writings of the apostles, and may include gratitude for the gift of reconciliation.

As for the general intercessions, the beginning is addressed to the people as a call to prayer. There follow petitions drawn from the proclamation of Scripture and the needs of all peoples. It is a prayer of the faithful, but not exclusively for the faithful. Here is a privileged moment for the community to transcend itself in prayer for others. This wide-angle vision is substantiated by the suggested order of petitions: for the church universal, for public authorities and the salvation of the world, for those oppressed by any need, for the local community. Think of including real needs (nuclear disarmament, energy conservation, curtailment of inflation, bread for a hungry world, environmental protection) and real people (couples and families, children and youth, the mentally or emotionally disturbed, single and divorced people, prisoners) who seldom come under the usual purview of many intercessory prayers.

Prayerful

This criterion comes necessarily at the end in order to complete our acrostic WORSHIP. In order of importance, it should come first. Liturgical planning has to do with facilitating—not programming, which is beyond our power—a religious experience for our brothers and sisters in Christ. Liturgical evaluation should first of all ask: was it a prayerful encounter with the living God? The over-all mood should be one of wonder and awe, of praise and thanksgiving for the giftedness of life, and of paschal joy. In order to acquire this spirit, we need to help people come to see that prayer is something one can share with others: at home in the family or with friends, in non-eucharistic services such as the highly adaptable Liturgy of the Hours. The criterion of prayerfulness is what differentiates Christian liturgy from nonreligious ritual as an encounter with the mystery of God. The process is a dialogue of prayer. The dialogue partner is the Trinity of Father, Son, and Spirit. The content is the paschal mystery of Jesus crucified and risen.

As a college student singing in the glee club, I heard the director confide one day that he could never pray at the "High Mass" on Sunday. With his rich musical background, he simply became so easily distracted with the choral dynamics that he lost a sense of worship. A similar predicament awaits those involved in liturgical planning and preparation. Worship is meant to be experienced and celebrated first of all, not evaluated and critiqued. Evaluation should not prevent us from entering into the mystery we are celebrating. It is rather a means to an end, whereby an imperfect people try to improve our worship so that it be more genuine and authentic, worship celebrated in Spirit and in truth (Jn 4:24).

CHAPTER 8

Is the Mass a Meal?

Like the American flag a few years ago, even the eucharist can be an emotional sign waved differently by two opposing viewpoints. To some, *sacrifice* is the proper description of the Mass; to others, it is a *meal*. And neither party wants any facile solution that says it is *both*.

The roots of the argument lie deep in the hostility between Protestants and Catholics over the past four hundred years. If Protestants emphasized a doctrine or practice, we were cool; if they denied it, we gave it headlines. The things we agreed on (charity, of course) almost got lost in the smoke of battle.

Protestants shuddered at the thought of novenas, vigil lights, monsignors, and Mass stipends. So the Baltimore Catechism had eight pages about indulgences and nothing about the priesthood of the faithful, a frequent Protestant theme.

Likewise, as Protestant reformers continued to stress, at times one-sidely, the meal aspect of the Lord's Supper, Roman Catholic theologians felt compelled to respond with a lopsided concentration on the Mass as sacrifice and real presence. This explains the continued reluctance in Roman Catholic circles to recognize the eucharist as a ritual meal and to accept this emphasis in the liturgy today.

What is needed is a complete theology of the eucharist which, first of all, presumes the presence of the Lord in what we are doing—otherwise everything else collapses—and, secondly, takes as its starting point the words and actions of the Mass. In this way we can easily see that: 1) the actions of the Mass are those of a *sacred meal;* 2) the words are a *thanksgiving* prayer (eucharist); 3) and the Mass' ultimate meaning is that of a *memorial sacrifice,* a representing of the Lord's death and resurrection.

Therefore, to emphasize the meal aspect, as does the rest of this chapter, is not to deny the Mass as a thanksgiving or the Mass as a sacrifice. All three aspects are present and deserve recognition.

Scripture Portrays the Eucharist as a Meal

What do the sources of revelation—the Bible and tradition—tell us about the basic shape of the eucharist as a meal? The original accounts of Paul, Mark, Matthew, and Luke show the eucharist originating at the Last Supper as a meal within a meal. The sacred actions of Jesus with the bread and wine take place during a Jewish Passover seder supper, or at least a festive meal. Many of the resurrection appearances of Jesus involve partaking in a meal. The most important statement about the eucharist in Saint John treats it as the bread of life—living and life-giving bread. And the most ancient name for the eucharist was "the breaking of the bread" (Acts 2:42,46; 20:7), a designation that highlights the banquet aspect.

Hence, many scripture scholars today see the eucharist of the early church as a continuation of the table fellowship Jesus shared with his discples and followers during his earthly life. It should be not different today. Indeed, we must not only assert the real presence of Christ in the eucharistic bread and wine, but also the reason for that presence: Christ is the head of the family who graciously invites us, his followers today, to share a pleasant meal with him.

Some years ago Dom Gregory Dix demonstrated that all liturgies of both the Eastern and Western Churchs exhibit a four-

IS THE MASS A MEAL?

fold action: the taking of bread and wine, the blessing or giving thanks, the breaking of the bread, and the sharing of the bread and wine.[1] These four-fold eucharistic actions are obviously those of a meal. Here's how they translate into today's liturgy:

taking of bread and wine = preparation of gifts
blessing or giving thanks = eucharistic prayer
breaking of the bread and
 = communion rite
sharing of bread and wine

Thus a meal structure forms the basis of our Mass.

The Symbolism of Eating Together

Besides being true to the church's earliest tradition, recovering the sign value of the eucharistic meal could also enliven the much-neglected devotional aspects of eucharistic piety. It is not *words* which appeal most deeply to the religious dimension of the whole person. The liturgy is not just words; least of all is it a lecture. It is action—*prayer in action,* ritual prayer.

The forms of bread and wine are not things isolated in themselves, but are part of the whole symbolic action whereby the risen Christ continues to give himself to his church. They should be eaten and drunk as bread and wine, as Jesus offered them to his friends at the Last Supper. To the extent that this eating/drinking-in-friendship is made apparent, the meaning of our encounter with the Lord will be more readily grasped. We are dealing with real symbols (signs, sacraments) which bring about what they symbolize.

Gregory Baum describes the phenomenon of sharing a meal as a medium for celebrating the mystery of Jesus' dying and rising:

1. Gregory Dix, *The Shape of the Liturgy,* additional notes by Paul Marshall (New York: Seabury, 1982).

> The Good News implicit in the eucharist is that God offers men redemption through common meals. The marvelous may happen when people eat together. Eating itself is redemptive in the sense that here a man acknowledges his need of food and, hence, of other people ... If we consider how a meal shared with others offers men redemption from their pride and individualism and opens them to the human community, ... we see that eating may indeed be sacramental.[2]

In other words, we may appreciate the meaning of the eucharistic meal in proportion to our ability to share any human meal.

Improving the Meal Symbolism

Here are some of the ways in which the meal dimension of the eucharist may be recovered in our day. We are basing these suggestions on the church's tradition as continued in the General Instruction and the Revised Order of the Mass (1969), issued by Pope Paul VI. This is the official statement on the proper celebration of the eucharist and is the result of four centuries of liturgical science and the mandate of Vatican II for the revision of the missal.

Visibility of the Bread and Wine

It goes without saying that if the bread and wine are important, they should be placed in a position of prominence both on the offertory table before the presentation of gifts and afterwards on the altar. This means they should be plainly visible to the congregation and not obscured by the sacramentary or microphone. It may help to use a large paten in the form of a plate and a glass flagon for the wine.

2. Gregory Baum, *Man Becoming* (New York: Herder & Herder, 1971) 71.

Bread Consecrated at the Same Mass

This has been a constant exhortation of every eucharistic instruction since Pius XII's *Mediator Dei* in 1947. It stands to reason that if the eucharist is a meal as well as a sacrifice, then the food we eat should be present to us on the table from the beginning of Mass. Ordinarily it should not be the consecrated bread reserved in the tabernacle for communicating the dying and for eucharistic worship apart from Mass. A little planning and forethought regarding the number of communicants can normally assure enough bread consecrated for each celebration of Mass.

Communion under Both Kinds

The General Instruction (no. 240) gives three reasons why communion is more complete when both the bread and wine are received: a) "the sign of the Eucharistic meal appears more clearly" (Jesus instituted the eucharist under the forms of both bread and wine); b) "the intention of Christ that the new and eternal covenant be ratified in his blood is better expressed" (the words of the institution narrative: "This is the cup of my blood, the blood of the new and eternal covenant"); c) "the relation of the eucharistic banquet to the heavenly banquet" is better exemplified.

There are four accepted ways of sharing the cup: drinking from the chalice, communion by intinction, the use of straws (papal Masses in Rome), and spoons (Eastern Church). Although communion with the cup or chalice may be fraught with hygienic dangers which could deter some, certainly its sign value far outstrips communion by intinction. Jesus said, "Take and drink."

Bread That Resembles Bread

There is a provision of the General Instruction which has been little heeded:

The nature of the sign demands that the material for the Eucharistic celebration *appear as actual food*. The Eucharistic bread, even though unleavened and traditional in form, should therefore be made in such a way that the priest can break it and distribute the parts to at least some of the faithful (emphasis added). (no. 283)

But, sadly, the situation has not changed much since a report published in *Worship* magazine a few years ago:

The fact is that, four years after the *Instruction*, 91 per cent of parishes in this country are continuing with the conventional bread which is stark white, paper thin, often shiny and plastic-like. In addition, very few celebrants are breaking the large host for distribution, even when it is practical.

Maybe one reason why celebrants are not breaking the large host for communion is that there simply is not much to break! Even if it's impossible to buy hosts that "resemble bread" as they should, a community can always bake its own unleavened bread, for which recipes abound.

Rite of Breaking

Of the four eucharistic actions of taking, blessing, breaking, and sharing, the breaking of the bread has fallen into almost complete de-emphasis, or at times even misinterpretation. The time for the breaking of the bread is not during the recital of the consecratory words of institution, but during the communion rite. Once again the General Instruction catechizes us on its meaning.

Breaking of bread: this gesture of Christ at the Last Supper gave the entire Eucharistic action its name in apostolic times. In addition to its practical aspect, it signifies that in communion we who are many are made one body in the bread of life which is Christ (1 Corinthians 10:17). (no. 561c)

It is not the body of Christ that is broken. It is rather a multiplication of the loaves all over again. Many people share one meal, one Christ, one love. They stop being isolated grains and become one bread in the Bread of Life.

The General Instruction further advises that the Lamb of God may be sung with repeated invocations or tropes for as long as necessary to accompany the breaking of the bread. Making more of a ritual of it would restore the meaning of the rite of "breaking"—one of the four principal actions of the eucharist.

Communion in the Hand

Of all the features which could lead to a recovery of the meal dimension of the Mass, the restoration of communion in the hand is most promising. Only misunderstanding and a lamentable absence of catechesis can make this manner of communion controversial. Communion in the hand is the most ancient practice of receiving communion and persisted in the church for the first eight hundred years of its existence until a general liturgical decline forced its discontinuance.

Transforming the Assembled "Body"

Perhaps the foregoing seems to be excessively preoccupied with rubrics and ceremonial detail. Therefore, let us recall that the greatest liturgical symbol of all is the actual Christian community at worship. Moreover, the biggest change is not only that of the bread and wine into the sacrament of the Lord's Body and Blood, but the transformation of the eucharistic assembly into the Body of Christ which is the church.

Nonetheless, it is through the symbolic actions of the liturgy that our worship happens. A balanced eucharistic theology which keeps the meal dimension in perspective can serve to restore or intensify the other aspects of the Mass: the meaning of the *community* of the faithful; the *call to action* as an outgrowth of the eucharist; and the *eschatological dimension*, that is, its reference to our final and eternal salvation.

The Meaning of the Community of the Faithful

The 1973 instruction *Immensae Caritatis* recognizes the Mass's role in creating a community when it gives the reason for sometimes receiving communion twice in the same day: the sacrament of the Lord's Body and Blood unites us not only with Christ but with one another as the fullest form of liturgical participation.

Through communion we take on a new relationship with the other members of the eucharistic assembly. Our "Amen" at communion is thus an affirmation of two things: first, belief that this is the living Body of Christ and that he is Savior; second, that we hereby become church, the whole Body of Christ, head and members. As Saint Augustine once said, "By the grace of the redemption, you yourselves are what you receive. You acknowledge this when you respond, 'Amen'. What you witness here is the sacrament of unity."[3]

Our reverence should extend not only to the eucharistic bread and wine, but also to our brothers and sisters with whom we are made holy and sanctified at communion.

Impetus to Action for Others

Recovery of the sign value of the eucharistic meal could also preserve us from an overly individualistic eucharistic piety: me-and-Jesus to the exclusion of others. Maybe we should reread the Acts of the Apostles in order to grasp the strong sense of social action and concern verging on the point of primitive communism: "They devoted themselves to the apostles' instruction and the communal life, to the breaking of the bread and the prayers" (2:42). No one can wholeheartedly enter into the eucharistic spirit of this community without becoming more aware of the great community "out there"—a world which cries for bread and justice, for healing and love.

Other features of the revised Order of Mass—the general

---

3. Augustine of Hippo, Sermon 272, as quoted in Daniel J. Sheerin, *The Eucharist* (Wilmington: Michael Glazier, 1986) 94–96.

intercessions, gifts for the poor, the sign of peace—also call us to social action insofar as these can express our responsibility to feed the hungers of the human family.

A Sign of Eternity Beginning

One reason for communion under both species is that is relates the eucharistic banquet more closely to the heavenly banquet. In other words, there is more to come. The greatest things Christ has promised us have yet to be fully revealed.

Surely, it is no coincidence that both the Hebrew Bible and the New Testament describe the joy of heaven with the imagery of a sumptuous messianic feast. The salvation we await and which is already at work in the world is depicted in terms of intimate union with the Lord at a meal where all will be assembled together. "Here I stand, knocking at the door. If anyone hears me calling and opens the door, I will enter his house and have supper with him, and he with me" (Rv 3:20).

CHAPTER 9

Toward a Spirituality of Daily Mass

Like a bombshell bursting amid the pre-Vatican II sacramental theology of 1949, "The Many Masses and the One Sacrifice" remains one of the most explosive essays of Karl Rahner. The Innsbruck theologian examined the average view on the celebration of Mass and its frequency as generally established in the nineteenth century. This common view held that the multiplication or repetition of Masses automatically led to an increase in glory given to God as well as greater sanctification of God's people, according to an efficacy closely bound up with a theory of the fruits of the Mass. These fruits were described as a general Mass fruit (*fructus generalis*) for the benefit of the whole church, living and dead; a special fruit of the Mass (*fructus specialis*) for the benefit of those for whom the Mass is offered in a special way, whether living or dead, to be applied by the priest celebrant; and a personal Mass fruit (*fructus specialissimus*) which accrued to the benefit of the priest himself. Rahner dismissed the theory of the fruits of the Mass as a medieval accretion introduced in the thirteenth century to justify the taking of stipends for private Masses. He does, however, outline a respectable theology supportive of Mass stipends without resorting to this theory, based on an earlier tradition of people providing the material gifts for the celebration of a given Mass.

At the heart of his argument Rahner attacked this common view on the frequency of Mass celebration insofar as it mistakes both the objective nature of the Mass and the attitude of the worshiping subject before God. The sacrifice of the Mass differs from the sacrifice of the cross in the nature of a sign, on the sacramental or liturgical sphere, an "unbloody sacrifice" in the words of the Council of Trent. The only possible increase to glorifying God could result from the self-oblation of the church which accompanies this real memorial representation of the once-and-for-all unique and complete sacrifice of Christ. In this way the outward expression of union with the sacrifice of the cross is filled with the inner reality of her self-offering of the church's members. Hence the authentic participation of the church is what should determine the frequency of eucharistic celebration.

In terms of the efficacy of the Mass toward sanctifying the church, this likewise depends on the devotion and inner self-oblation of those offering the Mass here and now. The only conceivable limitations of the efficacy of the Mass stem from human finiteness, since its intensive (effectiveness for the individual believer) and extensive effects (number of faithful who share in its saving grace) are infinite. It is rather the human receptive capacity, the corresponding dispositions and spiritual preparedness, which limit the graced effects of the Mass. Rahner proceeds to state the principle regarding the frequency of the Mass:

The general conditions of physical and moral possibility being presupposed, the sacrifice of the altar is to be offered as often and only as often as in it and by it what is in human estimation a greater measure of actual personal participation in the Mass as Christ's sacrifice is attained, a greater measure than would be achieved if Mass were said less often or more frequently. In other words, Mass must be celebrated as often as its repetition increases the *fides* and *devotio* of those taking part.[1]

Over thirty years later, in the wake of the post-Vatican II liturgical renewal, how often we still have to remind ourselves that what happens at Mass takes place not only on the table-altar of sacrifice, but on the altar of our own hearts, for every eucharist should be an act of re-commitment and dedication to share more deeply in the paschal mystery of Jesus Christ as we try to love the way he loves us.

The frequency of eucharistic celebration continues to be a highly-charged emotional issue. For example, one of the kindest things you could say about a deceased Catholic is that he or she was a daily communicant. Frequent participation at the table of the Lord has become a yardstick with which to measure the intensity of a person's spiritual life. Before going any further, let it be clearly stated that this writer has a profound respect and reverence for the eucharist. It is the sacrament of the Lord's Body and Blood, an anamnesis of the sacrifice of the cross. The Mass is the greatest of all sacraments which expresses and forms us as church, the Body of Christ. Furthermore, the very last thing we want is a return to the Jansenistic rigorism which plagued the church for centuries and which Pius X sought to reverse in his decrees advocating a more frequent reception of communion. The eucharist is more an aid to living the Christian life which sustains us in our pilgrimage to God than it is a reward, since of ourselves we would never be worthy enough or deserving. It is precisely this profound love for the eucharist which prompts these open words about something many concerned people are feeling and thinking deep down inside.

Here is the thesis. The over-celebration of the eucharist has led to an inflation of Masses. What is intended in the words of

1. Karl Rahner and Angelus Haussling, *The Celebration of the Eucharist* (New York: Herder & Herder, 1968) 91–92. This is the more expanded treatment of the original article which appeared in *Zeitschrift für katholische Theologie* 71 (1949) 257–317.

the Constitution on the Sacred Liturgy to be the "source and summit" of Christian life has become an isolated pinnacle, bereft of the rich life of prayer and worship and Christian witness which both leads to the eucharist and flows from it. By going with our most sublime form of worship every time, the eucharist is no longer perceived as a special experience to be celebrated with awe and wonder. To use a colloquial analogy, it is like going out to dinner so often that something extraordinary has become very ordinary and commonplace.

This development is at variance with the oldest strata of the tradition of the church. While there may be indications in the New Testament that the primitive church in Jerusalem celebrated a daily eucharist (Acts 2:46), the emphasis in the New Testament and early church was the weekly gathering on Sunday, the day of the Lord. For the early church it is helpful to make distinctions between daily prayer, daily community prayer, the daily reception of communion, and the daily eucharistic assembly.[2] Daily prayer was a way of living out the scriptural admonition to "pray always" (1 Th 5:17). Daily community prayer led to the development of a daily morning office (lauds) and an evening gathering for prayer (vespers), the nucleus of the Liturgy of the Hours which originated as a participatory public celebration in cathedrals and parishes. The practice of daily communion existed in the second and third centuries as people brought communion home with them from the Sunday eucharistic assembly so as to be able to communicate the "daily bread" of the Lord's Prayer during the week. The custom of daily eucharist is first attested to by Cyprian of Carthage (d.258), perhaps more as a family or domestic style of celebration. By the time of Augustine (d.430) the church in North Africa was celebrating a daily public eucharist. But daily

2. Robert Ledogar, "The Question of Daily Mass," *Worship* 43 (May 1969), 258–280. I am indebted in many ways to this insightful article. For a more recent treatment of this topic, see Robert Taft, "The Frequency of the Eucharist," *Beyond East and West: Problems in Liturgical Understanding* (Washington, D.C.: The Pastoral Press, 1984) 61–80; John F. Baldovin, "Reflections on the Frequency of Eucharistic Celebration," *Worship* 61 (1987) 2–16.

Mass was by no means a universal practice in the first five centuries of the Western Church, nor was it a universal ideal. Augustine himself urged flexibility and tolerance.

> As to customs which differ according to country and locality, as the fact that some fast on Saturday, others do not; some receive daily the body and blood of the Lord, others receive it on certain days; in some places no day is omitted in the offering of the holy sacrifice, in others it is offered only on Saturday and Sunday, or even only on Sunday, and other such differences as may be noted; there is freedom in all these matters, and there is no better rule for the earnest and prudent Christian than to act as he sees the church act wherever he is staying. What is proved to be against neither faith or morals is to be considered optional and is to be observed with due regard for the group in which he lives.[3]

The collapse of all prayer and liturgical activity into the Mass so that "liturgy" has come to be equated with "eucharistic liturgy" is a comparatively recent phenomenon which has come upon us through three factors. First, the provision for evening Masses has been so exploited as to effectively exclude any possible time allotment for other services of prayer and worship at night. Second, a lack of respect for the religious affectivity provided in popular devotions has led to their elimination under the mistaken guise of liturgical renewal. Third, we are only now beginning to see that we desperately need transition points or bridges between prayer alone and the eucharist. Such bridges today could be occasional Bible services of the word, opportunities for shared prayer, and the restoration of the Liturgy of the Hours, in particular morning and evening prayer, as a highly adaptable manner of common prayer which can sanctify and transform the day.

The over-frequent offering of Mass has impoverished the general liturgical life of the church. It has obscured the normative meaning of Sunday Mass. By way of an analogy of faith (as

3. Epistle 54 to Januarius: PL 33: 200; translated in the Fathers of the Church: *Saint Augustine, Letters,* I (1951) 253.

expounded by Aidan Kavanagh), a norm is a standard against which a given practice is measured; it has nothing to do with how often a thing is done.[4] Here are some examples. The theological norm for Christian initiation is the RCIA with the restored catechumenate; a pastoral adaptation of the theologically normative meaning of adult initiation is the religious education of children which works out to be a kind of post-baptismal catechumenate. The theological norm for the Liturgy of the Hours is a participated service of common prayer; a pastoral adaptation would be the priest or religious praying the breviary. The theological norm for the sacrament of penance/reconciliation is the forgiveness of serious sins after baptism; the pastoral adaptation is the tradition of devotional confession. Seen in this analogy of faith, the theological norm for the Mass is the Sunday eucharistic assembly, the self-actualization of the church as it comes together on the first day of the week, a little Easter, to remember the Lord as he wished to be remembered—in the "breaking of the bread." This should be kept in mind when scheduling Sunday Masses not for sheer personal convenience but because of a sense of theology of the local church which tries to bring together as many communicant members as possible under the one roof of the house of the church at the same time. A pastoral adaptation of the theologically Sunday eucharistic assembly is the celebration of Mass at other times during the week. Mass on Mondays, or Tuesdays, or any other day derives its meaning from the theological norm of Sunday. Without wishing to wax too subjective, we might occasionally ask ourselves what is it that brings us together to celebrate eucharist: Sunday, a feast day, an event of special significance for the local church or parish? Do we have a conscious reason for offering Mass, or has it become a routine devotional practice?

The misuse and abuse of the Mass has turned a sacrifice of praise and thanksgiving into an ascetical discipline of formation in Catholic schools and houses of religious formation. It is re-

4. Aidan Kavanagh, *The Shape of Baptism: The Rite of Christian Initiation* (New York: Pueblo Publishing Co., 1978) 108.

freshing to note that paragraph 27 of the Directory for Masses with Children cautions against daily celebration: "Weekday Mass in which children participate can certainly be celebrated with greater effect and less danger of weariness if it does not take place every day." What is the sacrament of the unity of the church has often become an exercise in private devotion and individualistic piety. It is useful to recall the underlying reason why one may under certain circumstances be permitted to receive communion twice in the same day is that the sacrament binds us more closely in communion with a different eucharistic assembly of our brothers and sisters in Christ. All of this has fostered an over-reliance upon the Mass as a ritual form for every conceivable purpose, at times when it may not be called for: for example, for large throngs of people in an unenclosed area; for Boy Scout award and graduation ceremonies; for funerals and weddings where conditions might suggest that a non-eucharistic liturgy would be more appropriate. Worse still, the Mass is used as a didactic tool for catechetical instruction.

The over-frequent celebration of Mass has impoverished the faith life of the people, leading to a general torpor and a jaded reverence. We might try to rediscover the vivid contrast still maintained in the Eastern Orthodox Church between fasting and feasting where the eucharist is not offered on a daily basis. The new missal of the Ambrosian liturgy of Milan likewise has kept the Fridays of Lent as aliturgical days with no provision for the celebration of the eucharist. Some years ago I participated in a symposium on Christian initiation conducted at the abbey of Senanque in southern France. Twice daily we celebrated non-eucharistic worship services adapting some of the features of the RCIA. By the time we celebrated the concluding Mass, where we renewed our baptismal promises, the participants had developed a true hunger and thrist for the bread of life and the cup of eternal salvation. The eucharist was experienced as the culminating point of our entire week; it had been recovered as the source and summit. Too many Masses can encourage a tendency to hide behind a very complex ritual form rather than share ourselves in prayer. It can lead to ennui and boredom when we take for granted what should be an act of grateful acknowledgment (*berakah*). It can deprive the people of God of other liturgical experiences which could widen their faith vision and stretch their life of prayer. So difficult is it to reverse this trend that most parishes that have genuinely attempted to introduce other services such as the Liturgy of the Hours feel compelled to integrate morning or evening prayer into a eucharistic celebration so as to ensure attendance.

The indiscriminate celebration of Mass has also taken its toll on the presbyteral ministry. Many priests, faced with daily bination—scheduled daily Mass and possible funerals, etc.—can become ineffectual leaders of prayer, simply going through the motions. The ministry of the ordained priest risks a one-sided sacramental or cultic orientation, to the neglect of the ministry of word and pastoral leadership. Already now in team ministries priests with excessive liturgical responsibilities are envious of lay associates who are free to be more pastorally present to people. In view of the declining number of priests, several options are open: either change the discipline so as to admit married men and women to the priesthood; or widen the liturgical presidency for some of the sacraments so as to include lay people (for example, anointing of the sick); or develop other liturgical services as has already been provided for in the helpful Directory for Sunday Celebrations in the Absence of a Priest, recently promulgated by the Congregation for Divine Worship, to aid assemblies in preparing celebrations held with a deacon or lay person presiding.[5]

This chapter has explored the theology underlying the frequency of eucharistic celebration and its tradition in the church. We have seen how the over-frequent celebration of Mass can lead to an impoverishment of the liturgy, a diminution of the faith life of the people of God, and an unbalanced ministry of the ordained priesthood. What is needed for the future is the

5. Congregation for Divine Worship, Directory for Sunday Celebrations in the Absence of a Priest (2 June, 1988), reprinted in *Origins* 18:19, (20 October, 1988. See also International Commission on English in the Liturgy, *Sunday Celebrations. Guidelines to Aid Assemblies in Preparing for Celebrations Held with a Deacon or Lay Person Presiding*. Second printing. March 1979.

kind of tolerance and respect for diversity of eucharistic practice and spirituality along the lines for which Saint Augustine pleaded. Where weekday Mass is continued, special attention might be given to the scheduling, the environment, and the ritual format. A misguided approach to Mass stipends should not be allowed to perpetuate some of the liturgical travesties which have taken place where Masses are booked by strangers for years in advance. The environment for weekday Mass should be markedly adapted to the smaller number of participants, either the faithful gathered around the altar in the sanctuary or, better yet, a special chapel for weekday celebration. It is also a fervent wish that a format for weekday celebration be developed, one that is vastly simplified from that on Sunday.

Reconciliation
and
Healing

The Key
CHAPTER 10
to the Sacrament
of Reconciliation

Someone recently asked me what I thought about "the sacrament of reconciliation." "Which sacrament do you mean?" I replied. "Do you mean baptism, the eucharist, or penance/reconciliation in the stricter sense? All three of these can lay claim to being sacraments of reconciliation."

Sacraments of Reconciliation

Since apostolic times baptism has been acknowledged as the premier sacrament of penance, conversion, reconciliation. At the conclusion of Peter's discourse on Pentecost Sunday the vast throng from all nations, visibly moved and brought to the brink of conversion by Peter's stirring words, asks what they should do. Peter responds: "You must reform and be baptized, each one of you, in the name of Jesus Christ, that your sins may be forgiven; then you will receive the gift of the Holy Spirit" (Acts 2:38). The one faith statement with reference to baptism in the Nicaeo-Constantinopolitan Creed we profess at every Sunday Mass is: "We acknowledge one baptism for the forgiveness of sins." The symbolism of the water bath itself is indicative of a cleansing from sin or, even better, a conversion which comes about from being plunged into the paschal mystery of Christ's death and resurrection.

What, then, is the relationship of baptism to penance? The Council of Trent in the sixteenth century referred to penance as the second plank (baptism being the first) after the shipwreck of sin. In other words, penance has to do with the remission of post-baptismal sins. Years earlier Saint Ambrose of Milan poetically described this relationship: the church "possesses both water and tears for the forgiveness of sins: the water of baptism, the tears of penance."[1] With the advent of the normative practices of infant baptism, a notable shift in emphasis has occurred: penance has become the conversion sacrament; confirmation the sacrament of commitment. It could be that many problems relating to a penance catechesis are more directly rooted in the process of Christian initiation. The sacrament of penance is a sacramental moment in the life-long conversion journey of a Christian begun at baptism whereby we are restored and re-integrated into our baptismal grace and commitment.

The eucharist is also a sacrament of reconciliation. This reconciling dimension encompasses more than simply the penitential rite at the beginning of Mass, which indeed can be misleading if one feels this is the only part of the Mass that has to do with the forgiveness of sin. Listen to the Lord's Prayer, the embolism which follows ("Deliver us, O Lord . . ."), the Lamb of God, the very words of institution over the cup ("the cup of my blood . . . shed for you and for all so that sins may be forgiven"). The whole Mass is a celebration of reconciliation, which is what the Council of Trent had in mind when it spoke of the Mass as an expiatory sacrifice. The same Council went on to say: "For by this oblation the Lord is appeased, he grants grace and the gift of repentance, and he pardons wrongdoings and sins, even grave ones."[2] How does the eucharist relate to penance? While the precise nature of this relationship contin-

1. St. Ambrose, Letter 41:12 (PL 16: 1116). Also cited in no. 2 of the Introduction to the Rite of Penance.
2. Conc. Trid. Sess. XXII, c.2 (DS 1743).

ues to remain a matter of theological discussion, one could say that the eucharist is the greatest of all sacraments, the source and summit of Christian life, the paradigm of all other sacramental encounters with the living God which result in healing and reconciliation. Penance, however, has but a single specific modality, namely the forgiveness of sin, serious sin after baptism, to which one could also add a secondary tradition which provides for confessions of devotion.

Evolving Stages in the Sacrament of Penance

Not only is there more than just one sacrament of reconciliation, there is also more than just one way of celebrating the sacrament of penance/reconciliation in the stricter sense. Four stages have marked the evolution of this sacrament in the Roman Church: the solemn canonical penance of the early church, the Celtic penitential discipline of tariffed penance, private auricular confession, and the three forms of sacramental reconciliation provided in the post-Vatican II Rite of Penance (1973).[3]

The solemn canonical (public) penance flourished especially from the fourth to the sixth century. It was reserved for grave sins—notably but not exclusively the triad of murder, apostasy, and adultery—and could be accorded only once in a penitent's lifetime. The penitential journey was an arduous process accompanied by the prayer and support of the church. First of all, the bishop formally enrolled the candidates in the order of penitents. The penitent was quite literally "excommunicated" from the assembly: the church distanced itself from the sinner, whose sins had wounded the holiness of the church, in order to help bring about the sinner's conversion and reconciliation. Months and even years were spent in the order of penitents, a period characterized by a spirit of expiation and satisfaction for sin expressed in prayer, fasting, and other penitential observances. The solemn reconciliation of the penitent to the com-

3. See Richard M. Gula, *To Walk Again: The Sacrament of Reconciliation* (New York/Ramsey: Paulist Press, 1984); James Dallen, *The Reconciling Community: The Rite of Penance* (New York: Pueblo Publishing Co., 1986).

munity took place on Holy Thursday through the imposition of hands by the bishop before the assembly of the faithful.

The positive advantages of public penance in the early church were three-fold: a sense of genuine conversion, the experience of the communal support of the reconciling church, and a realization that other ways of forgiveness were also open to sinful Christians. The sense of genuine conversion grew out of the entire process extended in time. Today we seem to have collapsed the whole conversion process, the doing of penance, and the celebration of reconciliation into the few moments of the sacramental encounter. The recovery of Lent as a penitential season of conversion and tentative efforts at restoring an order of penitents in parishes today present interesting possibilities for the future.[4] The communal support of the church was evidenced in the public liturgies and prayer for the repentant sinner. In the words of Saint Jerome, "God does not restore a member to health until all the members have wept for him."[5] The other ways of forgiveness were noted by Augustine who outlined three types of penance: the penance of catechumens preparing for Christian initiation at baptism; the daily penance of Christians who seek forgiveness in the Lord's Prayer; and "penance with tears" for the grave sins of those who participated in the order of penitents. On the debit side, the solemn canonical penitential discipline of the early church reached an impasse and ended in a pastoral failure because of its increasing rigorism and enduring aftereffects which frightened away most Christians until its reception on their deathbed.

The Celtic penitential discipline arose from a different corner of Western Christendom: the Irish monks who introduced it to

4. See the intervention of Cardinal Bernardin at the 1983 Synod of Bishops, "New Rite of Penance Suggested," *Origins* 13 (1983) 324–326. See also Robert Blondell, "Penance Today: A Possible Solution," *Assembly* 10 (1983) 219–221; James Lopresti, *Penance: A Reform Proposal for the Rite*, American Essays in Liturgy 6 (Washington, D.C.: The Pastoral Press, 1987).

5. St. Jerome, *Dialogue Against the Luciferans* 5 (PL 23: 67), as cited by Paul Palmer, *Sacraments and Forgiveness* (Westminster, MD: Newman, 1959) 110.

the European continent in the seventh century. The practice originated in monasteries, most likely as a form of lay confession; hence the ordinary minister was not the bishop but the presbyter or priest. Its liturgy was accordingly less solemn and public. "Tariffed penance" is another name for this development, since the presbyter imposed a penance or satisfaction on the penitent in keeping with a particular sin, condition, and state in life. The most important change is that now the penitential discipline was no longer unique and could be received more than once in a lifetime. At its best the Celtic practice was an instance of discernment of spirits, the prayer together of priest and penitent leading to sacramental forgiveness. Such continues to be the thrust of the first form of our present revised rite of reconciliation of individual penitents. At its worst, tariffed penance became an exercise in casuistry and legalism, attested to by the numerous penitential books of the age.

Private auricular confession was a further outgrowth and evolution of tariffed penance in the twelfth century. This is the sacrament which was the subject of the deliberations of the Council of Trent and is the only form most of us have known in our lifetimes. Its special features are the emphasis on the role of the priest as judge, a less harsh and severe satisfaction or penance, immediate reconciliation, and a paramount importance attached to the act of confession (hence the name). It should be noted that the acts of the penitent also comprise contrition and satisfaction. These acts of worship on the part of the penitent—contrition, confession, satisfaction—together with the prayer of absolution by the priest confessor form the sacramental sign. The penitent is not a passive recipient but an active co-celebrant of the sacrament.[6] Moreover, the root meaning of confession (*confiteri*) includes not only an avowal of guilt but also a profession of faith and an action of praise and thanksgiving for the goodness and mercy of God. For example, the famous Confessions of Saint Augustine were not a kind of sensational tabloid but are cast in the framework of a confes-

6. See Karl Rahner, "Forgotten Truths Concerning Penance," *Theological Investigations* II (Baltimore: Helicon, 1969) 135–174.

sion of faith praising and thanking God who had mercifully forgiven his sins. On the one hand, private auricular confession has proven to be a school for holiness for many persons seeking to grow in Christ. On the other hand, the almost total absence of a communal dimension have led some to call it "sacred therapy for the individual conscience" or "private spiritual therapy" at the expense of social responsibility and the experience of the church's involvement in the reconciliation process.

Revised Rite of Penance

A lively sense of the tradition of penance/reconciliation can help us understand the present stage of this evolving sacrament as found in the Rite of Penance. There are three modes of sacramental celebration, two of which are communal: Rite for Reconciliation of Individual Penitents, Rite for Reconciliation of Several Penitents with Individual Confession and Absolution, and the Rite of Reconciliation of Several Penitents with General Confession and Absolution.

The Rite of Reconciliation of Individual Penitents is an enrichment of the best features of the original Celtic practice. The priest representing the reconciling church invites the penitent to an experience of prayer together, discernment of spirits, which leads to sacramental forgiveness. It is because of this dynamism that the proper liturgical environment for celebrating reconciliation is essential, namely reconciliation rooms.

The Rite of Reconciliation of Several Penitents with Individual Confession and Absolution works best with smaller groups of a limited number of penitents and an adequate supply of confessors. An intrinsic structural problem often impedes its celebration from being either fully personal or fully communal. The personal dimension suffers when the penitent has scarcely enough time to blurt out one or two sins. The communal dimension is weakened when the service breaks in the middle for individual confessions with the ensuing time lapse before gathering together again for the conclusion.

The Rite of Reconciliation of Several Penitents with General Confession and Absolution is printed in the ritual as one of three liturgical expressions of the sacrament. It is, however, subject to the stringent provisions of paragraphs 31 and 34 of the Introduction: grave need, insufficient confessors, individual confession of serious sins afterwards.

All three forms of sacramental celebration exhibit a similar structure:

- reception and welcome
- proclamation of God's word
- confession of sin
- proclamation of forgiveness
- thanksgiving and praise

This similar structure permits a dialogue between the ministers and the people and enables the liturgical planners to shape the form of celebration according to such practical factors as the size of the community, environmental space, the need of the participants, and the number of priests available.[7]

Sin, Conversion, Reconciliation

What, then, is the key to the sacrament of reconciliation? It is illuminating to recognize that there are other sacraments of reconciliation such as baptism and eucharist. It is likewise liberating to know the four stages in the evolving tradition of the specific sacrament of penance/reconciliation. Hopefully we will thus be more freed up in discerning which of the present modes of sacramental or non-sacramental celebration is called for on a given occasion. But the real solution is to begin with the experience of sin, conversion, and reconciliation in Christian life and to see how these experiences are both framed and enlarged in the liturgical celebration.

A healthy sense of sin. Remember the film *Lovers and Other Strangers*? Recall the sequence showing the confessions after

7. See the helpful commentary by Nathan Mitchell, ed., *The Rite of Penance* III *Background and Directions* (Washington, D.C.: The Liturgical Conference, 1978).

the wedding rehearsal. The church-going mother of the bride launches into an endless laundry list of faults. The scene shifts to the other side of the darkened confessional where the father of the bride can only mutter "I didn't do nuthin." Neither the mother nor the father really confronted themselves as sinners, a realization that they were personally responsible for their failures to love. The fact of the matter is that we make mistakes as Christians; we fail to respond to the unconditional love of God. Sin is a breakdown of multiple relationships: with God, with others, within ourselves. In terms of our relationship with God, sin alters or weakens our fundamental choice or option: are we moving toward or away from God? Sin hurts other people. It is difficult to conceive how we could sin without in some way injuring others, either directly (for example, anger, hatred, irresponsible sex) or indirectly by participating in structures which exploit and oppress the poor and disadvantaged. Sin is also intrinsically self-destructive. We hurt ourselves when we sin, diminishing our human potential as sons and daughters of God.

I remember a story told on a college retreat in the 1950s of a young engaged couple striving to express their affection chastely before marriage. One night while parked on a lonely road, they go "too far." Almost immediately a trailer truck slams into the parked car killing the girl and institutionalizing her fiancé with a nervous breakdown resulting from a sense of guilt. Reflecting back, I can say now that this story was inappropriate both because of its wrong idea of sin (simplistic law and order mentality) and its wrong idea of God (the "god of the ambush" more interested in devising ways to condemn his creatures than in saving them). An Appendix to the Rite of Penance contains an examination of conscience which could guide us in conscience formation.

> Is my heart set on God, so that I really love Him above all things ... ? Have I a genuine love for my neighbors? ... Do I do my best to help victims of oppression, misfortune, and poverty? ... In my work or profession am I just, hardworking, honest, serving society out of love for others?

114

The novels of Mary Gordon and others remind us of our guilt-ridden past and an unhealthy sense of sin. The pendulum has now swung to the other extreme. The peril in contemporary society is that we adopt a Pelagian attitude which pretends that sin no longer exists.

The experience of conversion. It is an easy temptation to measure the value of our religious experiences by the intensity of how well we feel. The better we feel, the closer we seem to be to God; the easier it is to find God and to pray. The shallowness of this approach becomes apparent when we find ourselves unable to cope with and integrate difficult situations and trials into our following of Christ. Is God totally absent from periods of disillusionment, abandonment, helplessness, discouragement, depression, temptation, despair? Is there nothing we can discern from these with regard to our life in Christ and his community the church? Upon reflection we come to see that these seemingly negative experiences can be moments of conversion and growth wherein we learn three truths: about ourselves, about others, about God.[8] The truth about ourselves is that we discover within ourselves a conflict between a true self as created in God's image and a false self full of egocentric desires. Our life's task is an ongoing conversion of moving progressively from self-absorption to self-donation. The truth about others is that our own poverty of spirit and radical neediness lead us to a greater solidarity with others. Walls of isolation or imagined superiority/inferiority come tumbling down. No one has it all together. We share the same human condition in need of redemption. We come to a greater awareness of the interdependence that exists among the members of the Body of Christ. The truth about God is that we begin to experience God in a new way. Salvation, redemption, liberation, healing are just so many words and abstract concepts until we realize they are happening to us! I am being saved, redeemed, set free, healed! Jesus is my personal Savior. The mystery of his dying and rising is being relived in our very own flesh.

8. See Paul V. Robb, "Conversion as a Human Experience," *Studies in the Spirituality of Jesuits* XIV, no. 3 (May 1982).

The experience of reconciliation. How are people reconciled to-day: couples, families, friends, religious communities, and rectories? Reconciliation usually begins with the admission of wrongdoing and expression of sorrow: "I am sorry for what I said or did." There are words and actions expressive of a renewal of the relationship. Oftentimes these may be non-verbal: the tears welling up in the eyes of a child, the embrace of a couple. Some course of action is then designed to reverse the wrongdoing so as to reduce the likelihood of its happening again. Is not a similar process at work in the sacrament of penance when the acts of contrition, confession, and satisfaction (amendment) come together with the prayer of absolution to form the sacramental sign of forgiveness? Maybe we have to experience reconciliation first at a human level in everyday life in order to grasp what the sacrament of reconciliation is all about.

At the close of the Sixth General Assembly of the Synod of Bishops devoted to "Reconciliation and Penance in the Mission of the Church" Pope John Paul II stressed the importance of reconciliation among nations and the need for a penitential attitude among peoples, calling for a "contemporary penitential catechesis." In my opinion this is the key to the sacrament of reconciliation, even more important than the actual frequency of any one form of celebration. For example, the first form (auricular confession) can easily become a routine habit, just as the third form (general absolution) can re-enforce a magical mindset as if any sins could be forgiven without interior conversion. The sacrament of penance is intended to promote and intensify the spirit of reconciliation which makes up Christian life. Perhaps then we will be in a position to appreciate what it means to hear the words of Jesus: "Your sins are forgiven." This is what truly makes the Gospel "good news."

General Sacramental Absolution and the Symbolic Language of Penance

CHAPTER 11

Probably the most insightful exegesis of the Council of Trent's teaching on the integrity of confession has been the research of Fr. Carl Peter of Catholic University. Building on the research of scholars before him such as Piet Fransen, Peter readily acknowledges that concepts of "faith" and heresy employed by Trent have a much broader meaning than divinely revealed truth or its denial. For example, the fact that an "anathema" is attached to a certain statement does not always mean that such a position, or its opposite, is proposed as divinely revealed, that is, not necessarily *de fide definita* as understood by a later age. What then of Trent's celebrated canon 4 of the 14th session (1551) which insists that by divine law (*ex jure divino*) all mortal

117

sins are to be confessed according to number and kind? On the one hand, Peter rejects the assertion of some theologians that the material integrity of confession is a purely disciplinary law of the church. It is rather a divinely willed religious value. On the other hand, the integral confession of mortal sins according to number and kind is not such an absolute value that it must be present in every circumstance. At times other values may take precedence, for example, emergency situations as have always been recognized in the past or the contemporary need for a more communal and liturgical celebration of the sacrament. Peter concludes that the teaching of Trent does not rule out a possible change in the liturgical rite which would involve "only generic confession and communal absolution coupled with the obligation of confessing specifically within a definite period of time."[1]

But can one ask further: what is the theological reasoning behind Trent's insistence on the integrity of confession? Without having exhaustively combed the *Acta Concilii Tridentini*, I would tentatively suggest three possible theological avenues of approach behind Trent's doctrinal position.

The first line of approach has traditionally been a comparison of the sacrament of penance to a juridical tribunal with the priest confessor serving as judge. This view, popular among the Scholastics, would argue that justice can only be properly administered when the judge knows the particular malice of the sin (species) and how often the individual committed the

1. Carl Peter, "Auricular Confession and the Council of Trent," *The Jurist* 28 (1968) 297. This conclusion is remarkably similar to the solution ultimately adopted by the revised rite of penance. More recently Fr. Peter has expressed himself on this subject in "Integral Confession and the Council of Trent," *Concilium* 61 (1971) 99–109; "The New Norms for Communal Penance: Will They Help?," *Worship* 47 (1973) 2–10; "Dimensions of *Jus Divinum* in Roman Catholic Theology," *Theological Studies* 34 (1973) 227–50; and entries in the supplementary volume of the *New Catholic Encyclopedia*. See also *General Absolution: Toward a Deeper Understanding* (Chicago: Federation of Diocesan Liturgical Commissions, 1978) in which this chapter first appeared.

crime (number).[2] In response, a more contemporary theology would rejoin that the sacrament is primarily a celebration of God's mercy and that Trent used the juridical image only as an analogy—*ad instar actus judicialis* (after the fashion of a judicial act)—in order to refute the Reformers who seemingly denied the sacramental efficacy of the rite. God alone is the ultimate judge. The judgmental role of the priest confessor is to ascertain whether the penitent is properly disposed to receive absolution.

A more compelling theological reasoning behind the Tridentine integrity of confession would concentrate on the shape of the sacrament as then practiced in the sixteenth century, private auricular confession which had evolved from the earlier Celtic penitential practice. The abiding value of auricular confession, a kind of concelebrated sacrament, is the prayer of the priest and penitent together in order to discern the Spirit of God. This approach is substantiated by Chapter I (Rite of Reconciliation of Individual Penitents) of the revised sacrament and its introduction.

> In order to fulfill his ministry properly and faithfully the confessor should understand the disorders of souls and apply the appropriate remedies to them. He should fulfill his office of judge wisely and should acquire the knowledge and prudence necessary for this task by serious study, guided by the teaching authority of the Church and especially by fervent prayer to God. Discernment of spirits is a deep knowledge of God's action in the hearts of men; it is a gift of the Spirit as well as the fruit of charity.[3]

In other words, an articulation of the nature and times of sinful actions is important in order to uncover the core of the sinful

2. See Peter Mueller, C.P. and Edward Senior, C.P., "Canonical Confession in the Western Church," *Resonance* 2 (1966) 75–96 (special issue from St. Meinrad's School of Theology on Penance: The Ministry of Reconciliation).

3. Rite of Penance, no. 10/a. See also John Gallen, "A Pastoral Liturgical View of Penance Today," *Worship* 45:3 (1971) 132–150.

heart so that it in turn may be overwhelmed by the healing grace of Christ. This second approach to the abiding value of integrity of confession is very much in keeping with the teaching of contemporary moral theology on the fundamental option: in this case, a sinful attitude which expressed itself in outward actions.

There is also a third theological motivation behind the Tridentine doctrine of integrity: a liturgical argument which perhaps can only be fully appreciated in retrospect and which is the point of this chapter. Sacraments are not things or objects. They are symbolic encounters with the Risen Lord in his church, a sacramental dialogue with the very mystery of the Triune God, be this a baptismal bath of regeneration, a chrismal anointing with oil, a eucharistic meal. Without the participation of the recipient involving some symbolic exchange, there is no sacrament. In view of the limited liturgical manner of celebrating the sacrament of penance as Trent knew it, the confession of sins was necessary as the one symbolic manifestastion of the inner conversion of the sinner so as to ensure that a sacrament had in fact taken place. The Fathers of Trent were experientially unfamiliar with the public penitential discipline of the early church, which began with the admission of the sinful Christian into the order of penitents and culminated in the solemn reconciliation before the bishop on Holy Thursday. On that day the bishop or his representative would publicly reconcile the repentant sinner through the laying on of hands and the pleading intercessory prayer of the church (*supplicatio sacerdotalis*) which is always heard. The sacrament known to the Council Fathers was the medieval auricular confession: private, repeatable, with a satisfaction to be performed after, not before, the immediate reconciliation of the penitent. The Thomistic underpinnings of this practice as perpetuated in the revised rite of penance are that the interior acts of the penitent—contrition, confession, satisfaction—constitute the quasi-matter of the sacrament which go together with the priestly absolution, the quasi-form, to make up the single sacramental sign of penance.[4] Without the symbolic action of confession, the outward verbal expression of inner conversion, there would be no sacrament.

Without reverting to the public penitential discipline of the early church, the revised rite of penance has recovered many of its original liturgical features well worth preserving. Chapters II (Rite of Reconciliation of Several Penitents with Individual Confession and Absolution) and III (Rite for Reconciliation of Several Penitents with General Confession and Absolution) are cast in a communal format. Even Chapter I, the updated private auricular confession, which provides for the proclamation of the word of God, is imbued with a more liturgical setting. And restored to the very act of reconciliation—admittedly somewhat timidly and compromisingly—is the laying on of hands and a prayer of reconciliation phrased in both the conventional declarative ("I absolve you from your sins"—the medieval *Ego te absolvo*) and the primitive deprecative or epicletic ("through the ministry of the Church may God give you pardon and peace") mood.[5]

A similar liturgical development is also at work in the Rite for General Sacramental Absolution. Despite the restrictive features of paragraph 31 of the Introduction based on the Pastoral Norms of 1972, Chapter III stands alongside the other two chapters as one of three liturgical expressions of the one sacrament of penance.

Particular attention should be given to the insistence of Rite III on the gesture of the penitent requesting absolution, a gesture which may be further specified by the respective episcopal conferences by way of local adaptation.

---

4. See Rite of Penance, no. 6. Even the special terms *quasi materia quasi forma* indicate the particular exigencies of a sacrament whose symbolic exchange is a verbal one of confession. Furthermore, a tutorist position has always held that the sacrament, when received unworthily, did not revive.

5. Rite of Penance, no. 19, 46. See also James Dallen, "The Imposition of Hands in Penance: A Study in Liturgical Theology," *Worship* 51:3 (1977) 224–247.

The church's rich tradition, especially from the first centuries, has not been without its share of penitential symbolic actions expressive of an interior conversion of heart: for example, the rending of garments (indicative of a return to a primitive, disordered state because of sin), ashes and sackcloth (Ash Wednesday), fasting (Lent), bathing (baptism), pilgrimages, and the like.[6] Many of these are quite obviously culturally determined. More recently an FDLC paper has suggested possible symbolic actions for today whereby penitents may indicate their intention to receive general sacramental absolution:

Celebrant: Those who wish to receive the Sacrament of Penance are asked to give an outward expression of this intention and the proper dispositions. You may do so now by:

a) making the sign of the cross slowly and in prayer
b) bowing your head and praying for God's mercy
c) kneeling/standing in prayer for God's mercy
d) stepping forward as a gesture of your acceptance of God's mercy
e) receiving the imposition of hands (on those who have stepped forward)
f) joining hands
g) receiving the "light of Christ" from the Easter candle
h) receiving holy water and making the sign of the cross
i) responding aloud "Lord, hear my prayer" to the following

I intend to express sorrow for my sins, to try sincerely to change from my sinfulness, and to accept forgiveness and reconciliation from Christ through the ministry of the Church. In expression of this, we pray to the Lord:

Penitents: Lord, hear my prayer![7]

6. See P. Rouillard, "Quelques symboles, pénitentiels," in *Symbolisme et Théologie*, Sacramentum 2 (Rome: Editrice Anselmiana, 1974) 215–228.
7. Model for Provincial Guidelines on General Absolution, Form III.

These suggestions must be regarded as more than ceremonial refinements. They are attempting to find other, largely non-verbal, ways of symbolic exchange in the prayerful dialogue which makes up the sacrament of penance in whatever form it is celebrated. Where the integral confession of sins is rendered impossible, the very integrity of the sacrament demands we come upon other symbolic expressions.

Summary

The argument of this chapter has been a theological projection that whereas Trent was constrained to insist upon the material integrity of confession so as to ensure that a sacramental encounter had actually taken place in an otherwise aliturgical celebration devoid of further outward symbolic content may open the door to a realization that the always indispensable interior disposition of conversion may at times be expressed symbolically in ways other than words. Finally, what could be the positive outcome of this development?

First, the issue of the integrity of confession may be at last rescued from the exclusive juridical categories from which we never seem to let it become extricated. At the same time the positive value of confessing one's sins may be rediscovered, not as a dreary obligation, but as one of several sacramental expressions of inner conversion which is a special means of spiritual growth.

The very root meaning of "confession" may also be recovered. *Confiteri* not only means an avowal of guilt and sinfulness, it also implies a profession of faith (e.g., "confessor of the faith") and a prayer of praise and thanksgiving (*Confitemini Domino quoniam bonus est* = "Give thanks to the Lord for he is good.")[8] For example, Augustine's famous *Confessions* comprise that saint's profession of faith whereby he gratefully acknowledges the goodness of God who has graciously forgiven his sins. The sacrament of penance, as all sacraments, is thus per-

8. See J. Leclercq, "La Confession: louange de Dieu," *La Vie spirituelle* 118 (1968) 253–265.

ceived as a worship service of corporate prayer, as is especially underscored by the concluding "proclamation of praise" common to all three rites of the revised sacrament.

Third, this development could hopefully lead to a wider application of the symbolic actions of the penitent beyond integral confession. The misgivings with which many unfortunately surround the use of general sacramental absolution could be obviated. The first question which always seems to be asked is a juridical one: "Can you do it?" and not "Will it be of pastoral benefit to the penitent and the church?" One calls to mind, for example, those estranged or alienated from the church for a variety of reasons and who find it difficult at first to go to auricular confession. In view of the shortcomings of Form II, which is neither truly personal (too little time) nor communal (liturgical disintegration at the time for individual confession), we could come to use Form I and Form III more confidently as manners of celebrating God's forgiveness and reconciliation in the sacrament of penance which are not in competition but are complementary according to time, occasion and need.[9]

9. James Dallen, "Recent Documents on Penance and Reconciliation," in *Reconciliation: The Continuing Agenda,* ed. Robert J. Kennedy (Collegeville: The Liturgical Press, 1987) 95–113 details the growing restrictions placed on the use of Form III (general sacramental absolution). See the new Code of Canon Law, canon 961, and especially 960:

> Individual and integral confession and absolution constitute the only ordinary way by which the faithful person who is aware of serious sin is reconciled with God and with the Church; only physical or moral impossibility excuses the person from confession of this type, in which case reconciliation can take place in other ways.

See also the apostolic exhortation of John Paul II, "Reconciliation and Penance" (2 December, 1984).

Penance and the Anointing of the Sick

CHAPTER 12

In this chapter we want to review first of all the tradition of anointing of the sick. We shall then look at the theological issues, most especially the relationship between the sacrament of penance and anointing. Finally, we shall conclude with some pastoral applications.

The Tradition of Anointing

In the year 416 Bishop Decentius of Gubbio sent his deacon Celestine to Pope Innocent I to inquire about some pressing liturgical matters. Letter 25 contains valuable data about the evolution of "confirmation," penance, and the Roman Canon, and is especially helpful for our knowledge of anointing of the sick as practiced in fifth century Rome. The letter had far-reaching importance, being cited three hundred years later by Venerable Bede in England in 735, and would appear to reflect accurately the understanding and practice of anointing of the sick in the West for the first eight hundred years.

Your next question concerns the text from the epistle of the blessed apostle James: "Is any among you sick? Let him call for elders of the Church, and let them pray over him, anointing him with oil in the name of the Lord; and the prayer of faith will save the sick man, and the Lord will raise him up; and if he has committed sins, he will be forgiven." This must undoubtedly be accepted and understood as referring to the oil of Chrism, prepared by the bishop, which can be used for anointing not only by priests but also by all Christians whenever they themselves or their people are in need of it. The questions whether the bishop can do what undoubtedly can be done by priests seems superfluous, for priests are mentioned simply because bishops are prevented by other occupations and cannot visit the sick. But if a bishop is in a position to do so and thinks it proper, he, to whom it belongs to prepare the Chrism, can himself without hesitation visit the sick to bless them and anoint them with Chrism. But it may not be used on those undergoing penance for it is of the nature of a sacrament. How could one think that one kind of sacrament should be allowed to those to whom the rest is denied.[1]

Some comments are in order.

1. The practice is rooted in James 5:14–16, which Innocent quotes in full. There are some discrepancies however. James urges sick people to call upon the presbyters: if not priests as known today, at least office holders in the primitive church. Furthermore, James attaches more importance to the prayer of faith than to the actual anointing itself; the blessing of the oil itself goes unmentioned.[2]

2. The blessing of the oil was reserved to the bishop. The application of the blessed oil could be performed by presbyters and laypeople—and for that matter, bishops. Liturgical formu-

1. J. Neuner and J. Dupuis, *The Christian Faith in the Doctrinal Documents of the Catholic Church*, rev. ed. (New York: Alba House, 1982) 1603, p.450.

2. While the Council of Trent taught that the anointing of the sick was instituted by Christ and "recommended to the faithful and promulgated by James" (Neuner/Dupuis 1636, p.466), it was more nuanced in the third canon of 1551 suggesting that the rite and practice of extreme unction did not contradict the doctrine of James (Neuner/Dupuis 1658, p.471).

las for blessing oil are very ancient in the Latin Church, but not its application; rituals for the latter begin to appear only at the middle of the eighth century. Antoine Chavasse has exhaustively studied the sources available for the first eight hundred years: liturgical prayers of blessing, hagiographical accounts, and patristic writings. The thirteen extant prayers of blessing pray for wholeness of body, mind, and spirit; nowhere is anointing foreseen as a ministration for the dying. The blessed oil could be applied externally to the body or imbibed internally.[3]

3. The phrase "the nature of a sacrament" (*genus sacramenti*) refers to the blessed oil: it does not refer to the technical sense of seven sacraments as evolved in the twelfth century and first articulated by Peter Lombard, but rather something "hallowed" or made "holy."

4. Pope Innocent states explicitly that the anointing is not to be given to public penitents but only to the faithful in good standing. The implication is that it would also not be given to catechumens who were not yet baptized.

Thus we enter *in medias res* with the Roman pontiff who describes the established custom in the fifth century, based on the letter of James, which was the practice for the first eight hundred years. During the Carolingian renaissance of the ninth century a change occurred in pastoral practice and liturgy which was to profoundly transform the meaning of anointing from a rite for the sick into a sacrament for the dying. Various local synods show that as a result of the reform movement seeking to renew the priestly ministry, lay anointing was abandoned and the anointing of the sick was henceforth reserved to priests. Rituals for applying the oil were now for the first time created; previously the liturgical sources had to do only with the episcopal blessing of oil. The rituals for anointing came to be associated with the rites of deathbed penance,

3. Antoine Chavasse, *Etude sur l'onction des infirmes dans l'église latine du IIIe au XIe siécle.* Vol. I: *Au IIIe siécle á la reforme carolongienne.* The insights of Chavasse's unpublished second volume are available to us through Placid Murray, "The Liturgical History of Extreme Unction," *The Furrow* 11 (1960).

which was the usual occasion for sacramental reconciliation at that time. According to the tradition going back to Pope Innocent I, a sick person had first to be reconciled and in the good graces of the church before receiving the anointing. From this time onward two tendencies begin to mark the sacrament: a spiritualizing tendency associated with the penitential anointing of the five senses, and a growing perception of anointing as a rite for the dying. By the twelfth century the original order of penance, anointing, and viaticum had shifted to penance, viaticum, and anointing. Anointing had become quite literally extreme unction, the "last anointing."

This change in pastoral practice set the stage for the sacramental systematization of the Scholastic theologians. Anointing was numbered among the seven sacraments. Although some early Scholastics still maintained anointing was a sacrament for the sick, the consensus grew that it was impossible for the recovery of health to be a promised benefit of the sacrament infallibly bestowed. From its close association with death-bed reconciliation, anointing was thought to forgive sin. Since baptism removes original sin and penance remits actual personal sins, the sacramental grace of anointing was thought to pertain to the removal of either venial sin (Franciscan school of Bonaventure and Scotus) or the remnants of sin (Dominican school of Albert the Great and Thomas Aquinas). The purpose of the sacrament was to prepare the dying Christian for the beatific vision, an anointing unto glory.

The Council of Trent (1551) in refuting the Protestant Reformers affirmed that unction was a sacrament instituted by Christ, with an enduring salvific meaning which did not contradict the scriptural passage of James, for which the priest was the ordinary minister. But Trent declined to completely endorse the medieval approach to anointing as a sacrament for the dying. The original draft spoke of extreme unction as a sacrament to be administered "only (*dumtaxat*) to those in their final struggle and [who] have come to grips with death and are about to go forth to the Lord." The definitive text made a decisive alteration: "This anointing is to be used for the sick, but especially (*praesertim*) for those who are dangerously ill as to seem near to death." Three times the recipients of anointing were described as sick (*infirmi*), not dying. The Council taught that the specific effect of anointing was the grace of the Holy Spirit with spiritual, psychological, and physical ramifications.[4]

The post-Tridentine era, on the one hand, saw a progressive leniency concerning the interpretation of the danger of death required for unction and a gradual reassertion of anointing as a sacrament for the sick. Such teaching was reflected in the teaching of the Catechism of the Council of Trent and the encyclicals of Popes Benedict XV and Pius XI, who urged the administration of unction at the beginning of a "probable danger" of death. On the other hand, this century witnessed a resurgence of the Scholastic teaching regarding extreme unction as "anointing unto glory," preparing the soul of the dying Christian for the immediate beatific vision. This opinion, particularly popular in German dogmatic circles, held that granting the proper dispositions on the part of the recipient, the sacrament of unction has the power of canceling the total debt of punishment and thus preparing the soul for immediate entrance into heaven. One of the enthusiastic proponents in this country put it this way:

> Extreme Unction, if properly received, intends to eliminate purgatory for the recipient, intends to guarantee him the immediate beatific vision after death . . . Nor is there any reason to suppose that such a disposition should be particularly difficult to obtain. In the sacrament of Penance, ordinarily not all punishments are remitted. The Council of Trent (XIV Sess.) tells us that Penance will cleanse us perfectly only if accompanied *magnis fletibus et laboribus* [by many tears and much work]. This sacrament is therefore not available for our purpose. One might say that we have the plenary indulgence and the apostolic benediction. I answer that these depend too much upon the disposition, the piety and exertion of the patient. A plenary indulgence presupposes remission of all sins, and in so trying a need it is alto-

4. For a more extensive treatment of the Council of Trent, as well as the tradition of anointing, see Charles W. Gusmer, *And You Visited Me: Sacramental Ministry to the Sick and Dying* (New York: Pueblo, 1984) 3–47.

gether too uncertain a thing. We must have a sacrament; nothing else will do.[5]

This background is necessary in order to appreciate the theological issues at stake at the Second Vatican Council and the subsequent revision of the sacrament of anointing.

Theological Issues

There are at least three theological questions which have arisen regarding the sacrament of anointing since the Second Vatican Council.

First, is it a sacrament for the sick or for the dying? Here a remarkable evolution has taken place, greater than is generally observed. Paragraph 73 of the Constitution on the Sacred Liturgy represented a compromise. The name "extreme unction" was retained, but the Council Fathers thought it would be better called "anointing of the sick." The condition of danger of death (*periculum mortis*) still prevailed, but the sacrament should be celebrated at the beginning of the danger of death from sickness or old age. The breakthrough is found in the 1972 Latin typical edition, the 1974 provisional ICEL green book (translation), and the 1983 ICEL white book (translation and adaptation). Anointing is clearly the sacrament for the sick; the sacrament for the dying is viaticum, and one half of the ritual is devoted to this important and much-neglected sacramental ministry to the dying. Nowhere are the misleading terms "extreme unction" or "last rites" used; the name of the sacrament is "anointing of the sick" (*unctio infirmorum*). Furthermore, the condition for reception in the 1983 Pastoral Care of the Sick reads: the "faithful whose health is seriously impaired by sick-

---

5. F. Tecklenburg, "The Primary Effect of Extreme Unction," *Ecclesiastical Review* 55 (1966) 291–99. Paul Palmer, "The Purpose of the Anointing of the Sick: A Reappraisal," *Theological Studies* 19 (1958) 309–44 was one of the first in this country to challenge this approach.

ness or old age," a new rendering of the Latin *periculose aegrotans* previously translated as "dangerously ill."[6]

We mention in passing a second theological issue: what is the relationship of the sacrament of anointing to the charism of healing? If anointing is intended for sick people, what relationship does it have to the charism of healing expounded upon and practiced especially in pentecostal-charismatic circles today? To address these issues one needs to admit the similarities of the two ministries based on the ecclesial community's full commitment to minister to the sick and its use of varieties of ritual prayer to further this ministry. But a clear distinction between the two ministries must also be made on the basis of different modalities of prayer rooted in scriptural origin, their respective places in the church, and the expected results.[7]

The third theological issue with which we grapple is the relationship between penance and anointing. So much attention has been directed to the first two issues that this one still remains unfinished business. The brief survey of the tradition of anointing has surfaced the penitential aspects emanating from its association with deathbed penance which has profoundly shaped the history of the sacrament. A few examples will suffice. Until the revision in 1972 the essential sacramental sign consisted of the anointing of the five senses (matter) together with the words (form) first used in the tenth century: "May the Lord forgive you, by this holy anointing and his most loving mercy, whatever sins you have committed by the use of your [sight, etc.]." Another instance is the withholding of the sacrament of anointing from children. One popular moral manual explained the reason for this prohibition: "The subject must have attained the use of reason because Extreme Unction removes the consequences of sin, and one who has never had the use of reason has likewise never sinned."[8] Fi-

6. See Pastoral Care of the Sick: Rites of Anointing and Viaticum (Washington, D.C.: International Commission for English in the Liturgy, 1983).

7. See Charles W. Gusmer, "Healing, Charism and Sacrament," *Church* 2:2 (Summer, 1986) 16–22.

8. Heribert Jone and Urban Adelman, *Moral Theology* (Westminster, MD: Newman Press, 1962) par. 629, p.445.

nally, the refusal to allow deacons to anoint the sick is in part due to the sacrament's longtime association with penance, although there are other issues, most notably canon 4 of Trent that the *sacerdos* (bishop or priest) is the proper minister. Behind all this lurks a mentality vaguely alluded to by Tecklenburg in the passage cited earlier that anointing is a safer way to forgiveness of sins for someone seriously ill, inasmuch as penance requires a conscious subject capable of making acts of contrition, confession, and satisfaction.

What are we to make of all this? It is true that the teaching of the Council of Trent on anointing included penitential effects. Chapter 2 of that teaching stated that one of the results was that "anointing takes away the sins if there are still any to be expiated." Canon 2 anathematizes anyone who would claim that anointing "neither confers grace, nor remits sins, nor comforts the sick." By way of assessment and interpretation let this be said: anointing is a sacrament of the living. Its lawful reception presumes the state of grace and proper disposition. Where there is no other recourse (as with all sacraments of the living), serious sins can be remitted, but there is no forgiveness of sins without *metanoia* or conversion of heart.

Put more positively, a relationship does exist between penance and anointing, but not in the way this is usually conceived, as a remnant of the unfortunate association with deathbed penance and the subsequent Scholastic speculation. The relationship between penance and anointing is grounded in a holistic anthropology which views sickness within the wider context of the mystery of suffering and evil. This means three things.

1. Some relationship exists between sin and sickness. The Greek verb frequently used in Jesus' healing miracles is *sōzein* (to save), which can mean both salvation from sin and salvation from sickness and disease: "Your faith has saved you." James 5:15b ("If he has committed any sins, forgiveness will be his.") and the subsequent exhortation to mutual confession refer to a conditional effect of the rite. Herein is seen the close relationship between bodily and spiritual sickness and between physical healing and the forgiveness of sins. Many early church writ-

ers and the Council of Trent felt this passage referred just as much to the penitential discipline of the church as it did to the practice of anointing. It would also be an interesting project to reexamine the Scholastic teaching on original sin and the concomitant loss of the preternatural gifts of immortality, integrity, knowledge, and freedom from pain and suffering. In other words, sin—original and personal—has cosmic repercussions in terms of human solidarity and the ordering of the universe. This is not to say in a simplistic way that personal sin causes a given illness, an opinion reprobated by Jesus himself (Jn 9:3). Nor is this to state that sickness is a means of divine vindication, implying a "God of the ambush" waiting to get even! Rather, the whole human person in community suffers as a consequence of evil in the world.

2. The good news is that the promised salvation in Jesus Christ encompasses the total person in community with the goal of the resurrection of all flesh. Within this holistic vision of human history Jesus comes to free us, to heal us from sin and evil and all its manifestations, so that we can grow to full stature as children of God. In other words, God is on our side coming to save us.

3. Anointing of the sick is the complement or completion of Christian penance. This is not to be understood in the same sense that confirmation is the completion of baptism. Moreover, anointing is not given to persons because they are sinners or penitents but because they are sick. Anointing is the completion of penance not insofar as specified through sin but through sickness. Pain and suffering, accepted in faith and love, can purify a person more deeply from sin.

What is at stake here is a healthy concept of expiation. Suffering in and of itself has no value; suffering is ambivalent and can lead to either sin or to greater love. Moreover, God is not a sadist placated by the suffering of creatures. Recall also the opening paragraphs of the introduction to the anointing rite which refers to sickness as an evil to be resisted in the name of the kingdom of God.[9] Nonetheless, patient and courageous

9. Pastoral Care of the Sick nos. 1–4.

endurance of sickness can be a way of entering more deeply into the paschal mystery, experiencing poverty of spirit, dying to self-centerdness and allowing the risen Christ to penetrate our lives more completely. In his apostolic letter *Salvifici doloris* Pope John Paul II puts it this way:

> Suffering is in itself an experience of evil. But Christ has made suffering the firmest basis of the definitive good, namely the good of eternal salvation. By his suffering on the cross, Christ reached the very roots of evil, of sin and death. He conquered the author of evil, Satan, and his permanent rebellion against the Creator. To the suffering brother or sister Christ discloses and gradually reveals the horizons of the kingdom of God: the horizons of a world converted to the Creator, of a world free from sin, a world being built on the saving power of love. And slowly but effectively, Christ leads into this world, into this kingdom of the Father, suffering man, in a certain sense through the very heart of his suffering. For suffering cannot be transformed and changed by a grace from the outside, but from within. And Christ through his own salvific suffering is very much present in every human suffering and can act from within that suffering by the powers of his spirit of truth, his consoling Spirit.[10]

Pastoral Application

The three questions most frequently asked about the sacrament of anointing are these: Who may be anointed? Who may anoint? What does the anointing do? We answer these with special application to the relationship between penance and anointing.

Who May be Anointed?

Some clarity may be gained from the new Code of Canon Law which appeared after Pastoral Care of the Sick and thus represents the church's latest teaching on this matter.

10. John Paul II, "The Christian Meaning of Human Suffering," *Origins* 13:37 (23 February, 1984) 621.

Canon 1004: The anointing of the sick can be administered to a member of the faithful who, after having reached the use of reason, begins to be in danger due to sickness or old age.

Canon 1005: The sacrament is to be administered when there is doubt whether the sick person has attained the use of reason, whether the person is dangerously ill, or whether the person is dead.

Canon 1007: The anointing of the sick is not to be conferred upon those who obstinately persist in manifest serious sin.[11]

All this would seem to imply the following conclusions regarding the recipient of anointing.

Catechumens would not appear to be proper recipients of anointing. Although the church already cherishes them as her own, they are not yet *fideles* (faithful) through the sacrament of baptism, the gate to the church's sacramental life. In time of serious sickness, one might ponder if this is a moot question, since it might be more appropriate to celebrate first the initiation sacraments of baptism, confirmation, and first eucharist.

Penitents. Recall the teaching of Innocent I and the above-cited canon 1007. Penitents should first have recourse to the sacrament of penance and be reconciled with the church. No sins are forgiven without conversion of heart. The grace of anointing is not a blessing or a sacramental or the promise of a healing cure: the sacrament should not be received apart from a serious intention to live a Christian life. Anointing is not cheap grace, an easier way to have sins forgiven, or to save on medical bills!

Christians from other communions. Here the same conditions apply as for eucharistic sharing as set forth in canon 844 of the new code. There is a grave or pressing need, no access to one's

11. *Code of Canon Law.* Latin-English Edition (Washington, D.C.: Canon Law Society of America, 1983) 369. These canons have also necessitated some changes in the *Emendations in the Liturgical Books following upon New Code of Canon Law.* It is unfortunate that the Latin *periculum* was once again translated as "danger."

own minister, the person spontaneously requests the sacrament, commensurate faith, and proper disposition. Note that the Eastern Orthodox and Episcopal (Anglican) Churches regularly anoint their sick members.

Children who are ill. As we have seen, the penitential understanding of anointing is why the sacrament was withheld from small children: they are not yet capable of serious sin. One detects an opening in pastoral practice here. For example, Pastoral Care of the Sick contains some newly created sections devoted to sick and dying children. The emendations in liturgical books flowing from the new code now assert that children *are* to be anointed (earlier: may be anointed) if they have sufficient use of reason to be strengthened by the sacrament; in case of doubt whether the child has reached the use of reason, the sacrament is to be conferred.

Who May Anoint?

The penitential tradition of anointing is a partial reason why deacons are restricted from its administration. The question should ultimately be posed in the wider context of other pastoral ministers to the sick, both men and women. The current discipline is clear and is restated in canon 1003 of the new code: "Every priest, and only a priest, validly administers the anointing of the sick." Other doctrinal issues to explore would be these. First, we are dealing with an evolving sacrament, as is most evident in the progress made from the Constitution on the Sacred Liturgy to the recent revisions: from a sacrament for the dying to a recovery of its original meaning as a sacrament for the sick. Second, how is the *presbyter* of James to be understood and how open is the teaching of the Council of Trent to this development? Third, there already exist precedents for the extension of the sacramental ministry, for example, special occasions when priests may administer confirmation. Could this be applied to anointing when the church now encourages an earlier time for anointing but is unable in many parts of the world to provide priests to administer it? Fourth, there is the situation of ecumenical convergence, although here the practice varies: the Eastern Orthodox reserve the *euchelaion* or "prayer oil" to presbyters, indeed seven of them when possible; the American Episcopal Church permits the anointing by a deacon or lay person in emergency situations using oil blessed by a bishop or priest. Fifth, and at the root of all this, is a conflict between two theological principles: a sacramental *tutiorist* position whereby the church endorses the "safer" or surer theological opinion in matters pertaining to the salvation of its members (a particular concern here would be once again the penitential understanding of anointing restricting its administration to priests) and a pastoral principle that sacraments are for the people (*sacramenta propter homines*), and short of tampering with the substance of the sacrament every effort should be expended to make these means of grace available to people in need.[12]

What Does Anointing Do?

A rich ambiguity of expectations is described in paragraph 6 of Pastoral Care of the Sick and is actually a paraphrase of the teaching of Trent:

> This sacrament gives the grace of the Holy Spirit to those who are sick: by this grace the whole person is helped and saved, sustained by trust in God, and strengthened against the temptations of the Evil One and against anxiety over death. Thus the sick person is able not only to bear suffering bravely, but also to fight against it. A return to physical health may follow reception of this sacrament if it will be beneficial to the sick person's salvation. If necessary, the sacrament also provides the sick person with the forgiveness of sins and the completion of Christian penance.

12. The excellent study of John J. Ziegler, *Let Them Anoint the Sick* (Collegeville: The Liturgical Press, 1987) concludes that canon 4 of Session 14 of Trent "need no longer be considered an obstacle to the Church's appointment of someone other than an ordained priest as an extraordinary minister of the sacrament of the anointing of the sick" (p.6).

The Scholastic theologians spoke of the grace of unction as the forgiveness of venial sin/remnants of sin which prepared the dying Christian for the immediate vision of God. The grace was predicated on the assumption that the sacrament was intended for the dying and had the specific purpose of preparing them for heaven. This is indeed a beautiful and consoling teaching, but has to do with what we would now say is conveyed by the sacrament of penance and the apostolic blessing. If today we are returning to the earlier tradition that anointing is for the sick, the challenge presents itself: what, then, is the sacramental grace of anointing as the sacrament for the seriously ill? A more holistic anthropology is necessary and is captured in the revised liturgical action and liturgical word of the sacrament. The liturgical action (matter) consists of the anointing of the forehead and hands with the blessed oil, as well as additional parts of the body—the area of pain or injury. The liturgical word (form) during which the anointing takes place are these words incorporating the teaching of the Letter of James, the Council of Trent, and the earlier prayer of anointing:

> Through this holy anointing may the Lord in his love and mercy help you with the grace of the Holy Spirit. Amen.
>
> May the Lord who frees you from sin save you and raise you up. Amen.

We close with an excerpt from a graduate paper "Penance and Anointing" written by a talented priest, Kevin Duggan, whom I was privileged to teach. He looks at the relationship between the two sacraments from the perspective of Karl Rahner's theology.

> In addition to viewing the human from the nature/grace perspective, we can also speak of the human in terms of the nature/person question. By this we mean to say that the human being is essentially project at birth. For the believer, one's life can be seen as a journey or pilgrimage; it is a project in which one builds one's person within certain parameters set by one's na-

ture. The person grows as a person by disposing of oneself in free acts of knowing and willing always set within the horizon of God's call in grace. God is at one and the same time always the ground and horizon of human life, knowing and willing. This journey, one's life project, is one in which one faces obstacles; there is always the drag of one's nature which resists full disposition. Thus, the person under grace can be said to grow according to the law of gradualness. Two realities which are inherent within this human condition, with its gradual growth, are sin in its personal sense of actual sin and sin in its objective sense of the sin of the world. This sin of the world is ratified in personal sin, it is present in sinful human structures and too it is present in the experiences of suffering, illness and death itself which are experienced as unnatural, resulting from the effects of original sin. Where there is a certain naturalness to the aging process and death, it is experienced as unnatural, threatening, dreadful. These can also be seen within the context of the mystery of evil; without attempting a full theodicy, one can say that a person's life journey toward wholeness and holiness, the call of grace, takes place within this situation marked by sin. The journey is involved with overcoming the effects of sin within our hearts subjectively, and within our world objectively. Given this, the sacraments of penance and anointing are inherently related and complementary as "healing sacraments." As a sacrament of the living, one needs to be reconciled in order to be anointed, but the two function together in the intended health of the whole person. Their efficacious grace overcomes, in the person rightly disposed, sin and the sins of which we speak, as all sacraments in their soteriological orientation are involved with this overcoming of sin and the victory of grace. They are encounters with the living Christ, in the Church through the action of the Holy Spirit and the encounter occurs in the situation of one's life—a situation marked by the "limit" experiences of one's personal sin on the one hand, and of the fact of the sin of the world on the other—with its resulting human experience of illness, suffering and death. Grace seeks always to move one beyond the "limit" experience through overcoming the resultant alienation and thereby leading to greater integral human wholeness.

Through penance, we overcome the "limit" experience of our sinfulness and the process of conversion is furthered. The alienation which is sin gives way to the reality of reconciliation and greater wholeness. Through anointing, we overcome the "limit" experience of human suffering, illness and the eventual spectre of death which is part of any experience of serious illness. While bodily health may be restored, it is only for a time for we all must die. However, the grace of anointing with or without a physical cure aims at the cure of the person as a whole allowing for new possibilities of being this being-in-the-world and we thereby grow to greater integral, human wholeness. In this too, our life's project of building our person and making this person an offering to God in love is furthered.

In these "healing sacraments," in a special way, we are embraced by Love, an all-consuming Love; one which we experience, only in part, in our human loving and being loved—but one which we hope for in full in the eschatological fullness of the Trinitarian Love's embrace. It is the experience of sin and sickness, of alienation and suffering being overcome through prayer, faith and the sacraments which draws us further into the Mystery. The limit experiences of human life and love, under grace, open out into the limitless eternal love of the God who creates, redeems and sustains in love. In this the cry from the cross of our life with its sin, suffering and death is transformed from that of "My God, my God, why have you abandoned me" to the prayer and self-offering "Into your hands I commend my spirit."

CHAPTER 13

Healing: Charism and Sacrament

It is difficult to conceive of a more current and controversial topic among Christians than that of spiritual healing. The subject is of contemporary interest because of the current concern of the churches for healing, especially among pentecostal-charismatic groups, as well as the interest generated by the revised *Ordo Unctionis infirmorum eorumque pastoralis curae* (7 December, 1972), translated and adapted in the definitive ICEL version, Pastoral Care of the Sick: Rites of Anointing and Viaticum (1983). The theme of healing is also controversial because of the many attendant and theologically disputed areas, such as the mystery of suffering and evil (theodicy), the meaning of the healing activity of Christ (biblical exegesis), the abiding place of healing in the overall mission of the Christian church (ecclesiology), the relationship between sacramental and charismatic healing.

I want to begin with a consideration of human sickness in the light of faith; then consider the significance of Jesus' ministry to the sick; and conclude with an exploration of how this ministry is continued in the church today as a preeminently pastoral as well as charismatic and sacramental ministry.

The Phenomenon of Human Sickness

A wise physician once asserted that there is no such thing as sickness in itself, only people who are sick. This remark should serve as a safeguard against the danger of theologizing abstractly about human illness. Sickness is very real indeed.

The Human Person in His/Her Reality

Rather than resort to a kind of unconscious dualism that neglects the essential unity of the human person as a composite of body and soul, we might do well to return to a biblical anthropology that views the human person as an animated body, or to adopt a more contemporary theological approach toward the human person as a spirit in the world, an incarnate spirit. Applied experientially to the phenomenon of human sickness, illness profoundly touches and influences the total person. In addition to physical pain, the sick person endures psychic stress: isolation from family and profession; the impersonalism which even the best of hospitals can seldom avoid; the anxiety about "tests" and what the future may hold. When a person is seriously ill, the whole person suffers a disruption from the experience of life as it is normally lived. Serious illness also presents a temptation to one's faith in God: its ambivalence presents the occasion for either human growth and holiness or regression and possible despair. The Book of Psalms, the prayerbook of the Bible, vividly depicts this torturous and ambiguous plight of the sick (Ps 6, 32, 38, 39, 88, 102). As the Pastoral Care of the Sick succinctly puts it: "Those who are seriously ill need the special help of God's grace in time of anxiety, lest they be broken in spirit, and under the pressure of temptation, perhaps weakened in their faith" (no. 5).

142

Human Sickness and the Mystery of Evil

Although Jesus is careful to avoid too direct a causal relationship between illness and personal sin (Jn 9:2–3), it is nonetheless a biblical insight that some intangible relationship exists between cosmic sin and sickness, especially as illness is experienced today. The acute pain and often unrelieved anguish are the result of the sin of the world, a sinful disharmony in a creation that "groans and is in agony" (Rm 8:22) awaiting its deliverance. For example, Jesus frequently uses the word *sōzein* in his healing works ("Your faith has saved you"), which may refer either to salvation from sin, or from sickness and disease, or both. Or again, the prescription in the Epistle of James on anointing the sick is concluded with an admonition to repentence: "If he has committed any sins, forgiveness will be his. Hence declare your sins to one another, and pray for one another, that you may find healing" (5:14–16). Witness also the numerous exorcisms of the sick in the New Testament and the primitive church. Contemporary data from psychosomatic medicine seems to substantiate the claim that an intimate and inseparable connection exists between the human psyche and the body. In sum, the relationship between sin and sickness should not be misconstrued in a simplistic sense, such as that personal sin caused a given illness, or that sickness is the vindication of an angry deity who rains down chastisement upon disobedient children. Instead, the human person should be regarded as a historical whole who suffers sickness as a consequence of sin in the world, traditionally referred to as original sin. Two important conclusions follow. First, we should be careful not to blame God directly for sickness, as if God were its author. God reacts to and respects humankind's use—and lamentable misuse—of its freedom. There is a misunderstanding still deeply lodged in the hearts of many good people, who somehow revert to a "god of the ambush" instead of the New Testament revelation of a God of love called Father. Second, and very positively, the promised salvation in Jesus Christ is going to touch the total person, for its goal is none other than the resurrection of humankind (1 Cor 15). In this holistic vision of humankind, Jesus has come to free us, to heal us from sin and evil and all its manifestations so that we can grow to full stature as children of God.

Jesus' Ministry to the Sick

Jesus' ministry to the sick is one of healing in the widest sense of the word. He is presented at the outset of Mark's Gospel as a doctor come to cure an ailing human race (Mk 2: 17). In its ministry to the nations, the church very early recognized—and quickly rejected—a parallelism between Christ and Askleipius, the god of healing in the ancient world. This broad-based ministry of healing is evident in the account of the woman caught in adultery (Jn 8:1–11): a ministry of listening, for Jesus utters not a word until the end; a ministry of affirming ("Nor do I condemn you"); a ministry of freeing ("You may go. But from now on, avoid this sin"). Together with other scriptural images, such as reconciliation, justification, recapitulation, redemption (Redeemer), salvation (Savior)—healing (Healer) is synonymous with Jesus' life and ministry. If, therefore, human sickness is derivative from our alienation from God, healing is a divine reality which aims primarily at a wholeness before a transcendent God, a restoration or reconciliation which can bring about secondarily a temporal healing.

Jesus' Healing Works as Eschatological Signs of the Kingdom

On the one hand, we often labor under the inherited notion that a miracle is a supernatural act contrary to the laws of nature and hence an apologetic proof of divine intervention. To this must be contrasted the scriptural viewpoint that just as word and action go together in the revelation of God, so also do creation and salvation form a unity. Thus there exists a close similarity between nature miracles (calming the sea, for example) and healing miracles. A characteristic of the regin of Satan is Satan's hostility to creation. Lest Jesus be taken simply as a thaumaturgical wonder man, the Gospels generally avoid the terms miracle or wonder in preference for the more modest "acts of power" (*dynameis*) in the synoptics, "works" (*terata*) and "signs" (*semeia*) in John's Gospel.

On the other hand, the existence of the healing activity of Jesus of Nazareth is central to the New Testament. Mark's Gospel alone records over twenty individual acts of healing so that roughly one-half of his Gospel is given over to the healing narratives. In the Acts of the Apostles the witness of healing activity is likewise integral to Peter's kerygma on Pentecost Sunday (Acts 2:22) and elsewhere. In other words, the key question is not whether the healing works took place (which is assumed) or how they happened (possibly psychological suggestions in some instances), but instead what is their meaning.

The disciples of John the Baptizer approach Jesus to ask if he is the long-awaited Messiah who is to come (Mt 11:2–5). Jesus' response, invoking the imagery of Isaiah 35, contains an imagery that goes beyond physical healing: the blind are able to see the glory of God, cripples can walk in the path of God, lepers are cleansed of their sins, deaf people hear the good news, the dead are raised to true life in Christ, and the poor become rich through the preaching of the Gospel. Similarly the seven signs of the Fourth Gospel, three of which are healing miracles, have a deeper underlying meaning. For example, the man born blind (Jn 9:1–34) shows us that Jesus is the light of the world; the raising of Lazarus (Jn 11:1–44) points to Jesus as the resurrection and the life.

The healing works of Jesus are thus signs of the Kingdom of God, that central message of the New Testament that a new reign of peace and justice was at hand whereby God would put an end to the ancient enemies of the human race, sin and evil, sickness and death. The healing works of Jesus are eschatological signs in the sense of the "already" and the "not yet." The miracles foreshadow the ultimate transformation of humankind and the universe on the days of Jesus' Second Coming, the resurrection of all flesh, an event not yet come to pass. The blind man and Lazarus will eventually die, but the healing works on their behalf indicate, however briefly, something of the healing transformation that will take place on the last day. At the same time the healing miracles are eschatological signs of the "already" dimension of the kingdom at work in the world through the present offer of eternal life and communion with God which begins now in this life. Such appears to have been the understanding of the first Christians who transposed the healing gestures of Jesus into the rites of Christian initiation: exorcisms, profession of faith, *ephpheta* (Mk 7:34), anointing with oil (Mk 6:13), bathing in water (Jn 9), and the laying on of hands. In other words, the Risen Lord touches and heals now in baptism.

In passing, further similarities between the healing works of Jesus and the Christian sacraments may be observed. First of all, both bring about what they signify: the healing miracles are signs that announce the kingdom and usher it in; so sacraments signify the saving presence of God and also effect what they signify. Second, in both the healing experiences and the sacraments, the response of faith and conversion is paramount. Neither is magic nor automatic; the beneficiaries—the individual recipients and the witnessing community—are expected to behave as persons whose lives have been radically changed.

Paschal Mystery: The Healing Death and Resurrection of Jesus Christ

To all this must be quickly added that human wholeness is always a relative concept in this life. The ultimate healing transformation comes from suffering and death borne out of love. This is how the Kingdom of God advances. This is how Jesus became Risen Lord and how we, too, personally share in the Easter victory of Christ. This is what the paschal mystery is about, and Scripture could not be more explicit on this point.

The Risen Lord confronts and consoles the distraught disciples at Emmaus. "Did not the Messiah have to undergo all this so as to enter into his glory?" (Lk 24:26). He tells the doubting Thomas, "Take your finger and examine my hands. Put your hand into my side" (Jn 20:27). Even in his glorified condition the Risen Christ still bears the marks of his crucifixion.

An authentic Pauline mysticism strives for union with the crucified and risen one: a union that begins at baptism (Rm 6:3–11) and glories on the cross (Gal 6:14) as the only way toward full communion with the beloved. And while Paul graphically depicts the sufferings which come with his apostolate, the celebrated "thorn in the flesh" (2 Cor 12:7) would seem not to exclude the misery that comes from ill health. Far from a misguided spirituality that seeks to justify suffering for suffering's sake, and equally distanced from the opposite extreme which fails to see that Easter Sunday issues forth from Good Friday, Saint Paul captures the dynamic tension of sharing in Jesus' life-giving death and resurrection. "I wish to know Christ and the power flowing from his resurrection; likewise to know how to share in his sufferings by being formed into the pattern of his death. Thus do I hope that I may arrive at the resurrection from the dead" (Phil 3:10–11).

The message of the Fourth Gospel is similar: "Unless the grain of wheat falls to the earth and dies, it remains just a grain of wheat. But if it dies, it produces much fruit" (Jn 12:24). The driving force behind this ultimate healing through suffering and death is love. As John begins his account of the Last Supper and passion: "Before the feast of Passover, Jesus realized that the hour had come for him to pass from this world to the Father. He had loved his own in the world, and would show his love for them to the end." (Jn 13:1). The cross theology of John's Gospel further reveals that Jesus' "lifting up" on the cross—a turn of phrase that refers to the cross both as an instrument of torture and a way to exaltation—is the manner whereby Jesus will draw all people to himself (Jn 12:32). Finally, the blood and water flowing from the pierced side of the Lord are an indication that the crucifixion, resurrection, and outpouring of the spirit are intimately bound up together (Jn 19:34).

The introductory paragraphs to the Pastoral Care of the Sick (nos. 1–4), on human sickness and its meaning in the mystery of salvation, sum up this paradoxical predicament of Christian existence. On the one hand, we are challenged to struggle against sickness and seek the blessing of good health in the name of Jesus. And yet, on the other hand, there is a clear realization that the ultimate healing is not found in this life but comes instead from loving communion in the Lord's dying and

147

rising. To deny this would be to fall inadvertently into the hands of the very death-denying culture we are trying to evangelize.

The Church's Ministry to the Sick

Jesus' ministry to the sick is continued in his Body, the church. The Good Samaritan is the model of Christian compassion toward our suffering brothers and sisters (Lk 10:25–37). Jesus goes so far as to identify himself with the sick: "I was ill and you comforted me" (Mt 25:36). The church's mission in the world is to be a loving, healing, reconciling presence with special concern and affection for the helpless, the sick, the infirm, the aging. This overall healing ministry encompasses unpleasant social issues so easily glossed over in our Gospel preaching, such as better housing for the poor, more equitable distribution of food to the hungry, the critical need for energy conservation, nuclear disarmament amid a spiraling arms race, and so on. The church's ministry of healing should not be isolated or viewed apart from the rest of its mission to be a sign of Christ's continued presence in the world.

Pastoral Ministry to the Sick

"Every scientific effort to prolong life and every act of care for the sick on the part of any person, may be considered a preparation for the gospel and a sharing in Christ's healing ministry." (Pastoral Care, no. 32). More specifically, the church's pastoral ministry to the sick is practiced by all who care for the sick and dying at home, in the parish, and in hospitals. Through the ages this ministry has led to the foundation of Christian hospitals, as well as religious communities dedicated to caring for the sick. This pastoral ministry is also concerned about the spirituality and motivation of those involved in this work: doctors, nurses, families should know that they participate in the ministry of Christ to the sick continued in his church. Today especially there are hopeful signs of a rapprochement with the medical profession. In particular, cer-

148

tain psychologists (C. G. Jung and Victor Frankl) have been warmly disposed toward religion as providing a meaning to human existence so necessary in an often disturbed world. The pastoral ministry to the sick is not expendable and undergirds any further charismatic or sacramental ministrations.

Charismatic Ministry to the Sick

The Acts of the Apostles abound with instances of charismatic healing (Acts 6:8; 8:5–11; 10:38; 13:9–12; 15:12; 19:11–16). There is also strong evidence of a flourishing charismatic ministry in the early church as attested to by Quadratus (c.125), Justin Martyr (d.c.165), Tatian (c.160), Irenaeus of Lyons (d.c.202), Tertullian (d.c.220), and Origen (d.c.320). Some have attributed the waning of explicit charismatic healing activity to the rejection of the enthusiastic Montanist movement of the Spirit in the second century; others locate the slackening of charisms to a loss of spiritual vitality resulting from the conversion of Constantine and the advent of the cultural synthesis known as "Christendom." Nonetheless, traces of charismatic healing continued in the lives of saints and worthies, such as Martin Luther (d.1546), Philip Neri (d.1595), George Fox (d.1691), John Wesley (d.1791), Pastor Blumhardt (d.1880), and Father John of Cronstadt (d.1908). Charismatic healing is at work in shrines dedicated to the memory of the saints, Mary at Lourdes, for example, and in the provision for verifiable healings required in the canonization process. Although charismatic healing has therefore theoretically, at least, always been recognized, it is only in this century through the efforts of pentecostal and neo-pentecostal communities that this gift of the Spirit has been more fully restored to the church.

Sacramental Ministry to the Sick

Just as the charismatic ministry to the sick is to be situated within the context of the church's overall pastoral concern for the sick, so also is it to be exercised within the church's sacramental ministry. The eucharist as action (Lord's Supper) is a

149

representation of the healing power of the paschal mystery; as sacrament (communion) it is a pledge of the ultimate resurrection of the whole person (Jn 6). As charismatic communities may practice some form of exorcism or deliverance, a more common Catholic approach to healing would be the sacrament of penance, the healing sacrament directed per se toward the forgiveness of sins.

What is generally called the sacrament of the sick, however, is the anointing of the sick. In its recent revision it is no longer referred to as extreme unction, nor is it any longer a rite for the dying as such. Four reasons have prompted the Roman Catholic communion to revise the rite of anointing as a sacrament for those seriously ill from sickness or old age: scriptural evidence (Jas 5:14–15), the tradition of the anointing for the first eight hundred years, ecumenical convergence (practice of the Eastern Church and the Anglican communion regarding anointing), and the disappointing practice of a ministration people would postpone until their dying moments when they would no longer be capable of entering into the action of prayer.

The Rite of Anointing is described in these terms in its introduction:

> The celebration of this sacrament consists especially in the laying on of hands by the presbyters of the Church, the offering of the prayer of faith, and the anointing of the sick with oil made holy by God's blessing. This rite signifies the grace of the sacrament and confers it. (no. 5)

As is readily apparent, the sacrament is not without its moments of epiclesis—invoking the power of the Holy Spirit— both for the blessing of the oil and during its application upon the forehead and hands of the sick person:

> Through this holy anointing
> may the Lord in his love and mercy help you
> with the grace of the Holy Spirit. Amen.

May the Lord who frees you from sin
save you and raise you up. Amen.

Indeed, the very efficacy of the sacrament is attributed to the
sanctifying Spirit from whom various spiritual, psychological,
and even physical benefits may proceed:

> This sacrament gives the grace of the Holy Spirit to those who
> are sick: by this grace the whole person is helped and saved,
> sustained by trust in God, and strengthened against the tempta-
> tions of the Evil One and against anxiety over death. Thus the
> sick person is able not only to bear his suffering bravely, but
> also to fight against it. A return to physical health may even
> follow the reception of this sacrament if it will be beneficial to
> the sick person's salvation. If necessary, the sacrament also pro-
> vides the sick person with the forgiveness of sins and the com-
> pletion of Christian penance. (no. 6)

Distinction and Discernment

Charismatic and sacramental healing have many similarities.
They are situated within the community of the church, although a healer with a special charism or a presiding liturgical
celebrant may play a greater role in the service. They employ
similar gestures, namely, the laying on of hands, the sense of
touch conceived particularly as a way of bestowing or releasing
the power of the Holy Spirit. They are both—charismatic and
liturgical—first and foremost prayer: prayer of petition (charismatic "soaking prayer," sacramental "litany of intercession")
and prayer of praise and thanksgiving.

Why then a distinction between the two? This distinction,
in my opinion, is made on the basis of different modalities of
prayer rooted in scriptural origin, their respective place in the
church, and the expected results. Scripturally, charismatic healing takes its origin especially from the charismata listed by
Paul in 1 Corinthians 12: a gift with the community to be used
to build up the Body of Christ. Anointing of the sick finds its
scriptural precedent in James 5:14–15, where the elders or pres-

byters appear to be not simply men of advanced years or wisdom, but office holders or ministers in the primitive church. As Paul's description of the charismata is to be located within the total picture of his message to the Corinthians, so likewise it is helpful to recognize the background of James' letter. The author is advocating prayer as a response to various situations in which a Christian finds oneself, be this hardship, good spirit, or darkness—in which case the presbyters are to be summoned.

Regarding their respective place in the church, the church embraces both charism and institution, gifts and structure. The institution may appear to mirror more obviously the visible, tangible, incarnational side of the church, whereas the charism reflects more clearly the invisible, intangible, pneumatological aspect of the church. (Too great a split or cleavage should be avoided, for both come from God and should be animated by the spirit of Jesus.) It follows that charismatic healing partakes of the charismatic dimension, just as sacramental healing—in particular the anointing of the sick—is related to the church as its official liturgy on behalf of the sick.

Finally, concerning expectations that are focused on charismatic and sacramental healing, there seems to be a marked disinclination to predict results. Charismatic healing is often not instantaneous, and the grace of anointing the sick is described with a necessary ambiguity. Both involve expectant faith, although discernment of the Spirit should be undertaken as to what the praying community and the sick person can realistically expect. For this reason, for example, several optional prayers are provided in the anointing rite, depending on the condition of the sick Christian. In general, however, one could say that charismatic healing intends a cure, be this physical, psychological ("healing of the memories"), or spiritual (healing from sinful habits such as use of drugs, alcoholism, sexual abuse). Sacramental healing would appear to be less directly concerned with physical or emotional cures and aims at a deeper conformation with Christ through the healing power of the paschal mystery.

In conclusion, here are some suggested principles of discernment, especially applicable to any service of charismatic healing.

1. Does the service flow out of the local Christian community's ongoing pastoral care of the sick? More specifically, is the healing service a big extravaganza which crowds the church building on a given day, or is it an expression of an ongoing ministry to the sick and afflicted exercised by the church community?

2. Is the service pastorally responsible in terms of prior preparation and follow-up care? While an attitude of expectant faith should rightly be engendered, ministers preparing the participants should take time to present a sound pastoral theology of healing so as not to dash people's expectations or even shatter their faith when an immediate cure is not forthcoming. Similarly, one-night stands without any further pastoral care and attention would seem to be equally irresponsible and potentially disastrous.

3. Is there a sense of cooperation with the medical profession? Healing cures are not intended to spare patients medical bills; as is abundantly clear in the Gospels, they are intended to show forth the glory of God and to lead to conversion of heart.

4. Is there a proper emphasis on the worship of God and service of neighbor rather than a narrowly selfish therapeutic attitude which delights in the "miraculous"? The ministry of the sick, both sacramental and charismatic, has always been particularly susceptible to magical attitudes which would try to achieve a "quick fix" without getting at the deeper underlying Christian attitudes of surrender, trust, and love.

5. Are healings, whenever and wherever they occur, signs pointing to a deepened faith and conversion in which the beneficiaries are changed or transformed persons? Even more important than the physical or emotional benefits of Jesus' healing ministry was the fact that the people's lives were turned around and they became his disciples.

6. Is the approach imbued with the central mystery of the Christian faith, the passion, death, and resurrection of Jesus Christ and our participation in this saving paschal event? Saint

Paul has some very sharp words for those who are "enemies of the cross of Christ" (Phlm 3:18). His own personal confession of faith is one which every Christian is called to claim as well: "May I never boast of anything but the cross of our Lord Jesus Christ! Through it the world has been crucified to me and I to the world" (Gal 6:14).

Seasons
of the
Year

_____

Lent: Community Conversion

It has been a best selling book and a film seen by 135 million Americans. It has brought about a greater sensitivity to black culture and spirituality. Grandparents of all races and ethnic groups have suddenly become very popular figures sought out by their grandchildren who want to know where they came from. Airline commercials and newspaper advertisements urge us to discover our family history. In case you have not already guessed, we are talking about Alex Haley's epic work *Roots*.

As a Christian people we too have a need to discover our roots, our creative origins. We have to recover our true identity, where we as Christians come from. And we do this every time we celebrate the annual paschal mystery of Jesus' dying and rising in the season of Lent-Easter: a sacrament of time.

We should like to develop four theses:

1. Lent is a season of conversion and reconciliation.
2. Lent is a season of communal conversion.
3. The goal of Lent is Easter and the Easter season (Pentecost).

4. Lent is not so much what we are doing but rather who we are being as a Christian people.[1]

Lent: A Season of Conversion and Reconciliation

From the earliest times Lent has been a season of conversion, for this is how we begin and continue to share in the paschal mystery of dying to sin and selfishness and are raised up to a new life of grace in Christ. In the early church Lent was the privileged season for the initiation of new Christians and for the re-cycling of old Christians. Lent was a season for making new Christians, since the catechumens would embark on their final period of preparation of enlightenment prior to their reception of baptism, confirmation, and first eucharist at the all-night Easter Vigil service. Lent was a season for re-cycling old Christians, since the public penitents would be undergoing their Lenten observance preliminary to their reconciliation by the bishop on Holy Thursday. This need for conversion, expressed in the initiation of new Christians and the reconciliation of the old, persists today. In the Rite of Christian Initiation of Adults we have not a revision but a restoration of the catechumenate and reintegrated initiation sacraments for adults, which had virtually disappeared over a thousand years ago. This is the most radical of the post-Vatican II liturgical reforms, for the initiation of adults capable of a conscious faith response is clearly perceived as the theological norm of Christian initiation, which is coming to faith and conversion in the Christian church. What we do on behalf of children is a pastoral adaptation or application of the theologically normative adult initiation. Furthermore, the reconciliation of already initiated Christians has also been enriched by the revised Rite of Penance in its manner of celebration. The season of Lent is always an ideal time for the continued implementation of this sacrament, a kind of "second baptism."

1. The reflections in this and the following chapters have been corroborated by the circular letter concerning the preparation and celebration of the Easter feast, Congregation for Divine Worship, 16 January, 1988 (*Notitiae* No. 259, 24:2, February 1988, p.81–107).

These are the facts, the data. How can we make the liturgy of Lent come alive? Here is a projected Lent designed to make this season once again a time of conversion and reconciliation.

Ash Wednesday

What is urgently needed is less emphasis on the cosmetic and more on the kerygma! Ash Wednesday began as the day for the enrollment of sinners into the order of public penitents. This phenomenon later spread to all the faithful who came to realize the ongoing need for conversion in every Christian life. Ash Wednesday continues to remain a summons to parish renewal and conversion in the season of Lent. The ashes are always to be distributed in a faith context which includes the proclamation of Scripture and the prayer of blessing. Ideally the palm of the previous year could be burned publicly as part of the ceremony to show the continuity of the Lent-Easter season. And in my opinion the inevitable confusion on the part of many between the time of signing with the ashes and the time for communion would seem to suggest a celebration distinct from Mass. Two exhortations are provided for the distribution of ashes: "Turn away from sin and be faithful to the Gospel" (Mk 1:15) seems to be more in keeping with the Lenten season, whereas "Remember man you are dust and to dust you will return" (Gn 3:19) stresses more the aspect of human finiteness than a call to conversion.

First Sunday of Lent

The account of the temptation of Christ in the desert, reminiscent of the forty years' wandering of Israel, connotes decision, commitment. The first Sunday of Lent is the time for the Celebration of the Rite of Election of Catechumens and of the Call to Continuing Conversion of Candidates Who Are Preparing for Confirmation and/or Eucharist or Reception into the Full Communion of the Catholic Church, which is generally conducted at the cathedral by the bishop of the diocese. Prior to this, a Parish Celebration for Sending Catechumens for Elec-

159

tion and Candidates for Recognition by the Bishop may take place at Sunday Mass as the candidates begin their final period of preparation. The Rite of Christian Initiation of Adults puts it this way: "Adults are not saved unless they come forward of their own accord and with the will to accept God's gift through their own belief. The faith of those to be baptized is not simply the faith of the Church, but the personal faith of each one of them and each one of them is expected to keep it a living faith" (no. 211). For the faithful as well, the first Sunday of Lent, which originally marked the beginning of the Lenten season, points the way to the annual retreat in the church year, a true desert experience to draw close to the Lord and to renew the grace of their initiation sacraments.

Second Sunday of Lent

The Gospel today is always a proclamation of the transfiguration of Christ. His face changed in appearance, his clothes became dazzlingly white: all of this a foreshadowing of his Easter triumph. We also share in this mystery of transfiguration-transformation. We also share in the glory, the *doxa* of Jesus. There are two ways of conceiving this transfiguration in our lives. On the one hand, transfiguration means our humanization, the perfection of our human nature with Jesus as our model and exemplar: the glory of God is the human person who is completely alive. On the other hand, transfiguration also means our sanctification, our sharing in the divine life of God as adopted sons and daughters of the Father in the Son: "By the mystery of this water and wine may we come to share in the divinity of Christ who humbled himself to share in our humanity.[2] On this Sunday the penitential rite may be celebrated to mark the Lenten purification of the baptized but previously uncatechized adults who are preparing to receive the sacraments of confirmation and eucharist or to be received into the full communion with the Catholic Church.

---

2. Prayer for mixing of water with wine adapted from an ancient collect.

Third Sunday of Lent

The readings (Ex 13:3–7; Rm 5:1–2; Jn 4:5–42) from the A cycle of the lectionary, which may always be used for the third, fourth, and fifth Sundays of Lent, climax in the account of the Samaritan woman at the well. This is the time for the first scrutiny of the catechumens, which takes place at Mass and consists of an invitation to silent prayer, intercessions for the elect, an exorcism, and the dismissal of the elect. (Remember the old designation for the liturgy of the word: Mass of the catechumens?) The purpose of the scrutinies is aptly described in the RCIA as "meant to uncover, then heal all that is weak, defective, or sinful in the hearts of the elect; to bring out, then strengthen all that is upright, strong, and good" (no. 141). The abiding image of Jesus as the *living* water who slakes our thirst is carried over into the assigned preface of the eucharistic prayer:

When he asked the woman of Samaria for water to drink,
Christ has already prepared for her the gift of faith.
In his thirst to receive her faith,
he awakened in her heart the fire of your love.

Fourth Sunday of Lent

Today's readings (1 Sm 16:1–6, 6–7, 10–13; Eph 5:8–14; Jn 9:1–41), which are always the place to locate any discernible "theme," culminate in the cure of the man born blind. Stop to consider how the imagery and gesture of the healing miracles of the Gospels have been carried over into our liturgy of initiation: *touching* (laying on of hands), *bathing* (baptismal bath), anointing with oil, anointing with saliva (ephpheta rite), *exorcism*, profession of faith, and the like. Jesus is the light shining amidst the darkness of the world. We are bathed in his own wonderful light at baptism which enables us to see. The second scrutiny conducted today focuses on baptismal enlightenment or illumination: the various levels of conversion whereby we see with the eyes of faith (cognitive aspect), walk in the light of Christ (moral aspect), and come to contemplate the divine light (mystical aspect).

> He came among us as a man
> to lead mankind from darkness
> into the light of faith.[3]

Fifth Sunday of Lent

Today's readings (Ez 37:12–14; Rom 8:8–11; Jn 11:1–45) are especially appropriate. The raising of Lazarus highlights Jesus as the resurrection and the life, both for the catechumens preparing for the initiation sacraments at Easter on this third scrutiny Sunday and for all the faithful already initiated who continue to share in the eucharist, the repeatable sacrament of Christian initiation. All this should serve as a constant reminder that the salvation we long for is not only a spiritual entity but also encompasses the whole person who will be raised up. The Christian message of salvation is not exhausted in the immortality of the soul but includes the resurrection of all flesh. This cosmic dimension of the Christ event is alluded to in the preface:

> As a man like us, Jesus wept for Lazarus his friend.
> As the eternal God, he raised Lazarus from the dead.
> In his love for us all,
> Christ gives us the sacraments
> to lift us up to everlasting life.

Passion/Palm Sunday

Here is a rare opportunity for a procession of the entire congregation, not just the usual ministerial procession, from the place of blessing the palms to the church. The people's participation is further enhanced by the dramatized reading of the passion, a manner of proclamation that deserves greater atten-

---

3. Preface for the Fourth Sunday of Lent.

tion and use throughout the church year. For that matter, all of Lent should be directed towards an enriched participation of the congregation in worship, especially through the skillful use of nonverbal symbolic actions: palms that can be mixed with local greens by way of adaptation; water which provides a bath of immersion at the Easter Vigil or with which the people are truly sprinkled after their renewal of baptismal promises; the light service of the Easter Vigil which demands an appropriate hour of celebration; the oils blessed by the bishop at the Chrism Mass which could be suitably brought in the procession of gifts at the Holy Thursday Mass of the Lord's Supper; the bread and wine which are both offered to the communicants.

Finally, if Lent is to be a season of conversion, *metanoia*, change of heart, provision should be made for a communal celebration of the sacrament of penance at the beginning of Holy Week, as well as to ensure that the Easter Vigil always includes the initiation of adults, the reception of baptized Christians into full communion, or at the very least, the baptism of newly born infants. When celebrated properly, the abiding grace of the Lenten liturgical process should be that conversion takes time, is not instantaneous, and is, even less, automatic. Considering, for example, the "quickie" confessions of our recent past, we come to appreciate the richness of the revised rite of penance which would seem to assume a more developed, albeit, less frequent celebration.

This same extended manner of conversion is verified in the restored catechumenate, and for adults already initiated, a realization that Christian life is an ongoing, life-time conversion process, to be renewed especially every year at Lent. Lent is a season of conversion and reconciliation: a sacrament of time.

Lent: A Season of Communal Conversion

The RCIA puts it this way:

The period of purification and enlightenment, which the rite of election begins, customarily coincides with Lent. In the liturgy and liturgical catechesis of Lent the reminder of baptism already

163

received or the preparation for its reception, as well as the theme of repentance, renew the entire community along with those being prepared to celebrate the paschal mystery, in which each of the elect will share through the sacraments of initiation. For both the elect and the local community, therefore, the Lenten season is a time for spiritual recollection in preparation for the celebration of the paschal mystery. (no. 138)

Elsewhere, the RCIA (no. 75) describes the catechumenal catechesis as a multi-dimensional growth into a communal faith which is at the same time doctrinal, prayerful, apostolic, and communal. In this respect the catechumenate is thus a model or paradigm for all Christian formation, which to be effective and lasting, must be simultaneously doctrinal, prayerful, apostolic, and above all, communal. Let us apply these criteria to what a parish can do during Lent.

Doctrinal Instruction

This implies an updating of what we as Catholic Christians believe, which seems to be the evident concern of *Sharing the Light of Faith* (National Catechetical Directory). The findings of various polls conducted throughout the country seem to indicate that people may be rejecting a faith or theology which is no longer being proclaimed or taught, at least in circles where news of Vatican II has reached. What we are talking about is adult formation, which should also comprehend prayerful, apostolic, and communal features. The late Johannes Hofinger wisely depicted this need as a kind of concurrent pre-evangelization or evangelization.

Prayer

We stand in desperate need for bridges, points of transition, between prayer alone, evidenced by the immense interest in meditation, the Jesus Prayer, etc. and liturgical prayer, as exemplified, although not exclusively, in the eucharist. As far as a variegated expression of prayer, we seem in some instances to have been better off some years ago when one could point to weekly novenas and devotions which supplemented the liturgical diet. Carl Dehne keenly discerns the appeal of such services in the past:

> The devotions are designed for the kind of person who would rather visit a tomb or touch a cross than read a really good paragraph on the Paschal Mystery; who, when he thinks of the kingdom, wonders how he will know his friends there rather than how the mechanics of the omega point will be managed.[4]

In other words, the noble simplicity urged by the liturgical renewal need not necessarily imply a loss of affectivity in worship. Another bridge between prayer alone and liturgical prayer during Lent would be celebrations of the word (paraliturgies), especially with children and young people. These offer several advantages: a welcome relief to an overuse of the Mass as a sole ritual form of worship; they are open to creative experimentation; and the celebrant or leader of prayer need not be an ordained priest. Still again, shared prayer opens up another horizon. At first closely identified with the charismatic-pentecostal renewal, such a sharing of faith should be more widespread and acceptable if the Christian church is to endure in an age of secular pluralism.

A recently reintroduced point of transition would be the Liturgy of the Hours, beginning (morning prayer/laudes) and ending (evening prayer/vespers) of the day. Such was the origin of the cathedral or parochial office before the advent of monasticism and the subsequent privatization of the breviary. We should be particularly attentive during Lent and Holy Week to occasions which lend themselves to the implementation of this highly adaptable form of communal prayer.

4. In John Gallen, ed., *Christians at Prayer* (Notre Dame: University of Notre Dame Press, 1977) 94.

Apostolic Works

In addition to continuing traditional Lenten observances promoting self-discipline and union with Christ, we should also engage in endeavors which are both outward directed—the original idea behind fasting is that what you saved would be given to the poor—and communal, instilling a sense of church as mission. One very topical and current project would be to explore and implement, as far as possible, the teaching of John Paul II in his encyclical on social concerns (*Sollicitudo rei socialis*), as well as the U.S. Bishops' pastoral letters on peace and economic justice.

Communal Dimensions

When one considers the various biblical images used to describe union with Christ (the Johannine vine and branches, the Pauline Body of Christ: head and members), one is struck by an awareness that they all involve other people. Conversion is not something you do on your own in isolation. Aidan Kavanagh has wisely described the task of catechesis as "conversion therapy" whereby the community of the church enables you to survive a conversion experience. Furthermore, these images are organic, alive, showing growth, development, change, and necessarily suffering. If Lent is to be a season for communal conversion and reconciliation, the parish must also devote itself to reconciling polarized factions within its midst. Maybe the Italian-Americans can teach us something through their custom of exchanging palms on Palm Sunday with anyone they may have offended during the year. In the long run, the issue at stake in the reform of the church is not who is right, conservatives or liberals, but whether we have all experienced a conversion of heart.

Under the wider dimension of communal conversion, something should also be said of the diocesan community during the season of Lent. Here would be an opportunity to introduce stational liturgies at which time the bishop, following the lead of the bishop of Rome, would visit the parishes of his diocese.

Nowhere is a bishop more of a bishop, an *episcopus*, an over-seer, then when he observes the injunction of the RCIA:

> The bishop, in person or through his delegate, sets up, regu-lates, and promotes the program of pastoral formation for cate-chumens and admits the candidates to their election and to the sacraments. (no. 12)

And if the bishop is unable to preside at the sacraments of initiation, at the very least he is expected once a year to cele-brate the eucharist with the newly baptized (no. 251).

Finally, one diocesan liturgy of the Lenten season reserved to the bishop is the Chrism Mass with its blessing of oils. In order for this celebration to be a true celebration of the entire local church in its role as a priestly people, care and attention should be given to a proper time for scheduling, a better relat-ing of the blessing of the oil to those who will later benefit from its application (catechumens, recently initiated, confirmands, the sick and those who minister to them) and an opportunity for a re-commitment to ministry, not only for the ordained priests but for all ministries active in the diocese.

Nor should the wider ecumenical community be neglected during the season of Lent. This would be an ideal occasion for communities working and praying closely together to enter into some convenantal relationships. Towards our Jewish brothers and sisters we must also show a greater sensitivity to any possible anti-semitic polemical overtones of the passion narrative or other Lenten readings.

To conclude this second thesis, the catechumenal model of the RCIA reveals the paradigm of all Christian education: a multi-dimensional growth in faith which is comprehensively doctrinal, liturgical, apostolic, and communal. This model thus provides the criteria with which to evaluate the various Lenten processes designed for the whole parish which draw their in-spiration from the liturgical books of the Roman Rite.

The Goal of Lent Is Easter and the Easter Season (Pentecost)

A pilgrim to the Holy Land in the fourth century began the entry in her journal on Lent with these words: "Then comes the Easter season (*dies paschales*) and this is how it is kept."[5] In other words, Lent is not a self-contained season, isolated in itself. From start to finish, the goal of Lent is Easter, more specifically the Paschal Triduum beginning with the evening Mass of the Lord's Supper, reaching its high point in the Easter Vigil, and closing with vespers on Easter Sunday. As a matter of fact, in the revised Roman calendar Holy Week no longer exists as a liturgical entity; the season of Lent continues directly into Holy Thursday, at which time the Easter Triduum commences. If Lent is to be a season of communal conversion, it is because this is how we as church experience the paschal mystery, dying and rising in Christ. The entire Lenten season is a preparation for Easter, our yearly pasch as a Christian people. Here are two pastoral suggestions aimed at restoring the centrality of Easter.

First, make the Easter Triduum the center of the church year. Already from the very beginning of Lent on Ash Wednesday advertise the Triduum as the goal of our Lenten observances so that people will be able to renew their baptismal promises with a sense of genuinity and authenticity at the Easter Vigil and Easter Sunday. Urge people to keep the days of the Triduum relatively free in order to celebrate Easter properly. What a shame that many good church people might only come from Sunday to Sunday, thus missing out on the most important liturgy of the church year. And make the Easter Vigil, the mother of all vigils and the single most important liturgy of the year, more of a vigil gathering for prayer awaiting the resurrection of the Lord. Above all else, be sure to have candidates prepared for the sacraments of initiation.

Second, restore the continuity of Lent with the Easter Season. Even when Lent is celebrated as a season of communal conversion, all too often in the best of parishes everything

5. John Wilkinson, ed., *Egeria's Travels* (London: S.P.C.K., 1971) 128.

seems to shut down on Easter Sunday. We pray the words of the Easter preface "We praise you with greater joy than ever in this Easter season" but we do not appear to really mean it. One way to begin to restore the integrity of the Easter season would be to ponder carefully the assigned readings from the lectionary: the Johannine Gospels which promise the Spirit; the Acts of the Apostles which glowingly portray the activity of the Spirit in the primitive church. The Easter season is not just fifty days of celebrating the reality of Jesus' resurrection. It also celebrates the enduring meaning of this resurrection event, namely, our sharing in the life of the risen Lord through the Easter gift of his Spirit. We celebrate this gift of the Spirit not just at Pentecost, the climactic fiftieth day, but rather through-out the entire fifty days of Easter.

Another direction towards the recovery of the Easter season is provided by the Fathers of the church in their mystagogical catecheses, sermons given to the newly initiated during the Easter season.[6] Before the sacraments of initiation at the Easter Vigil, the Fathers seem especially intent on bringing the candidates to a conversion of life. After the candidates' initiation the Fathers take the Easter season as an opportunity to explain to the newly initiated the enduring significance of what happened when they were baptized, confirmed, and first communicated. The application for us today should be obvious. The particular way that life in the Spirit, the Easter gift of the risen Lord, happens for us is through our baptism. The Easter season is the pre-eminent time for a consciousness-raising of the ongoing meaning of the sacrament of baptism which should consistently determine our lifestyle as Christians.

Being a Christian People

We possess a number of fine inherited Lenten practices: prayer, not just saying prayers but a sense of the pervasive presence of God; fasting and abstinence as we follow Christ;

6. See Edward Yarnold, *The Awe-Inspiring Rites of Initiation* (England: St. Paul Publications, 1971).

almsgiving, better translated as a concern for others; the social action of a caring Christian community which would mark our Lenten observance. All of these practices should be expressive of an interior conversion of heart. They are not so much values in themselves as they are a response to the transforming action of God at work in our lives.[7]

In other words, Lent is not an onerous burden, an exercise in justification by works, but rather a grace to let the Spirit of God inwardly renew us. Or again, Lent is not the only time we work at being a Christian in community—it is possible to exaggerate its importance to the detriment of the rest of the church year—yet Lent is a microcosm of what it means to be a Christian people.

We see at long last what the Vatican II reform has been about from the beginning. What the paschal mystery of Jesus Christ really means, and why we have a season of Lent-Easter in the church year. Nothing less than the conversion of the church at the local level of the parish community. This is also how we as a Christian people recover our roots, for we as church were reborn from the pierced side of the crucified and risen Lord (Jn 19:31–37).

---

7. In this regard the apostolic Constitution on penance of Paul VI, *Paenitemini* (12 February 1966) deserves to be reread and consulted. See Austin Flannery, ed., *Vatican Council II: More Postconciliar Documents* (Northport, NY: Costello Publishing Co., 1982) 1–12.

Celebrating the Easter Season

CHAPTER 15

Even when Lent is properly celebrated as a season of communal conversion, all too often in the best of parishes everything seems to shut down tight as a drum after the last Mass on Easter Sunday. Publishers flood the market with all kinds of Lenten programs, but who ever heard of a program of renewal for the Easter season? We pray the words of the Easter preface: "We praise you with greater joy than ever in this Easter season," but our hearts are not really in it. And the fifty days of Easter are even longer than the forty days of Lent!

There are a number of reasons for this neglect. First, the liturgical calendar is the one liturgical revision overlooked and currently in the greatest need of more adequate catechesis. Far from simply designating when a given feast or season is to be celebrated, the church year is a "sacrament of time" which celebrates the mystery of Christ and his saints.

A second step toward recovering the integrity of the Easter season is to realize that Lent and Easter are two sides of the same coin: the one preceding (Lent as the Easter penitential season) the annual Paschal Triduum; the other issuing forth

171

from it. The Easter season was originally called Pentecost (Greek from "fifty"), a fifty-day time period which constituted a single feast day focusing on the unitary theme of Christ's passage from death to glory. Even the austere Tertullian described the mood of this season as one of unrestrained joy: the penitential signs of fasting and kneeling at prayer were set aside; the sung Alleluia ("Praise the Lord" in translation) was a mainstay. Spatial images further re-enforced a sense of expansiveness, boundlessness, freedom, and even eternity. This conception of the fifty days of Easter as a single unit of time continued well into the fourth century when the secondary tradition of Pentecost began to take root. No longer was Pentecost taken to mean fifty days, but rather the culminating fiftieth day itself which commemorated the coming of the Holy Spirit upon the apostles. By the seventh century the original approach grounded in John's Gospel with its unitive vision of crucifixion, exaltation, and outpouring of the Spirit bound up together in a theology of the cross had given way to the more historicizing tendency of Luke/Acts (forty days to Ascension, fifty to Pentecost).

The revised calendar does retain traces of this secondary tradition of Pentecost: "the weekdays after the Ascension to Saturday before Pentecost inclusive are a preparation for the coming of the Holy Spirit" (no. 26). But the overall thrust favors the recovery of the integrity of the original fifty days of the Easter season. The Sundays following Easter Sunday are no longer enumerated as Sundays *after* Easter but are called Sundays *of* Easter. Easter Sunday itself *is* the First Sunday of Easter. The Easter candle, an image of the risen Lord, is to be displayed in a prominent place and kept lighted for the entire fifty days, no longer extinguished on Ascension Thursday. The superfluous and misleading octave of Pentecost has been suppressed. And the very nomenclature Sundays or time after Pentecost has been more accurately replaced by ordinary time or time of the year.

There is yet a third reason for the confusion surrounding the Easter season. The Lent-Easter cycle has to do not only with the transformation of time, but as indicated in the sacramentary

172

and lectionary readings is intimately associated with the initiation of new members into the church. It is a baptismal season of conversion for initiating new Christians and recycling the old. The Easter season in particular should be marked by a postbaptismal catechesis or mystagogy, a continuing progression into the newly appropriated mystery of Christ celebrated in the liturgy. The Rite of Christian Initiation of Adults provides some guidance here: "This is the time for the community and the neophytes together to grow in deepening their grasp of the paschal mystery and in making it part of their lives through meditation on the Gospel, sharing in the eucharist, and doing the works of charity" (no. 244).

Let us take each of these three aspects in developing patterns for the celebration of the Easter season.

Meditation on the Gospel

To begin with, the weekdays of the octave of Easter, which are accorded the highest liturgical precedence as solemnities, call for the various Gospel accounts of the resurrection. As the Paulist Ordo eloquently puts it:

> The fifty days of Easter form one solemn feast, what Athanasius calls "The great Sunday." The days of Easter week form the "early hours" of this day, with accounts of the Lord who rose early in the morning, and the early preaching of the disciples who were witnesses to his resurrection.

As for the readings for the Sundays and feasts of the Easter season, Adrian Nocent has compiled a handy outline.[1] The RCIA (no. 247) suggests the proclamation of the A cycle readings from the lectionary in any given year because of their appropriateness for the newly initiated.

---

1. Adrian Nocent, *The Liturgical Year*. Vol. 3: *The Easter Season* (Collegeville: The Liturgical Press, 1977) 147–151.

Easter Sunday: "Christ is risen"
Acts: We ate and drank with him after he had risen (Acts 10:34a, 37–43)
Apostle: Look for the things that are above (Col 13:1–4)
                          or
          Be a new leaven (1 Cor 5:6b-8)
Gospel: *Morning:* Jesus risen from the dead (Jn 20:1–9)
          Evening: They knew him in the breaking of bread (Lk 24: 13, 35)
                          or
          Gospel of Easter Vigil

Sunday II: "The community believers grew; doubting Thomas"
Acts: The community of believers (Acts 2:42–47)
Apostle: Rebirth through the risen Jesus (1 Pt 1:3–9)
Gospel: Jesus appears on Sunday evening (Jn 20:19–31)

Sunday III: "The risen Christ appears to his followers"
Acts: Sermon of Peter on the risen Christ (Acts 2:14, 22–28)
Apostle: Redeemed by the blood of the lamb (1 Pt 1:17–21)
Gospel: They knew him in the breaking of bread (Lk 24:13–35)

Sunday IV: "The Good Shepherd"
Acts: Sermon of Peter: Jesus is Lord and Christ (Acts 2:14a, 36–41)
Apostle: We are healed and have come back to our Shepherd (1 Pt 2: 20b-25)
Gospel: Christ the Sheepgate (Jn 10:1–10)

Sunday V: "Ministries"
Acts: Seven men chosen who are filled with the Spirit (Acts 6:1–7)
Apostle: The royal priesthood (1 Pt 2:4–9)
Gospel: Christ the Way, the Truth, and the Life (Jn 14:1–12)

174

Sunday VI: "Expansion of the community"
  Acts: Imposition of hand and gift of the Spirit (Acts 8:5–8, 14–17)
  Apostle: Christ dead and risen is our hope (1 Pt 3:15–18)
  Gospel: Promise of the Spirit (Jn 14:15–21)

Ascension:
  Acts: Account of the Ascension (Acts 1:1–11)
  Apostle: Christ seated at the Father's right hand (Eph 1:17–23)
  Gospel: All power is given to Christ (Mt 28:16–20)

Sunday VII: "Witnesses to the Son: glory of Christ; prayer of Jesus"
  Acts: Prayer of the community (Acts 1:12–14)
  Apostle: Insulted for the name of Christ (1 Pt 4:13–16)
  Gospel: Father, glorify your Son the Christ (Jn 17:1–11a)

Pentecost:
  Acts: They were filled with the Spirit (Acts 2:1–11)
  Apostle: Baptized in the one Spirit into a single body (1 Cor 12:3b-7, 12–13)
  Gospel: I send you, receive the Spirit (Jn 20:19–23)

Participation in the Eucharist

The RCIA provides no special rites for the Easter season. The eucharist, the sacrament which completes baptism and confirmation and is itself a repeatable initiation sacrament for all Christians, is to be experienced as the source and summit of Christian life. Here are some ideas to highlight the Sunday eucharistic assembly.

Gathering Rites

The blessing and sprinkling with holy water as a baptismal reminder may be celebrated on each of the Easter Sundays as the principal element of the introductory or gathering rites at

Mass, incorporating the entrance song and procession (which occur during the sprinkling) and replacing the penitential rite. The blessing could take place at the main entrance to the church, preferably in close proximity to the baptismal font or even utilizing the font. The water should be contained in a worthy vessel, perhaps of glass or crystal for reasons of visibility. The prayer of blessing proper for the Easter season is found in the sacramentary. Perhaps even more appropriate than blessing the holy water anew each Sunday of Easter would be to adapt the present prayer as a kind of invocation over the water blessed at the Easter Vigil, a procedure similar to that suggested for the blessing of the water of baptism during the Easter season. An evergreen branch with short needles can facilitate the sprinkling which the people should experience as coming down upon their heads rather than splashing them in the face. The presiding celebrant may be assisted by a deacon or other ministers who may also sprinkle the blessed water so as to ensure that this symbolic action is performed in a generous way in which the entire assembly shares. The faithful should feel comfortable with this baptismal reminder and know that the appropriate response as they are being sprinkled is to bless themselves with the sign of the cross.

Liturgy of the Word

The assigned Gospel readings for the Easter season are taken primarily from John's Gospel with its Good Shepherd passages, the precious words of the last discourse, and the promise of the Spirit. The overall protrait of Jesus which emerges from John's Gospel is a more Easter-like Christ, as if already exalted as Lord during his earthly life. The Fourth Gospel is a more reflective one than the synoptics and demands a special manner of proclamation. The first readings, normally from the Hebrew Scriptures during the Sundays of the Year, are drawn from the Acts of the Apostles, which in the words of John Chrysostom present "the clearest demonstration of the power of the resurrection." On Sundays the middle readings from the Apostles are selected from 1 Peter (cycle A), which represents a primitive baptismal catechesis; 1 John (cycle B) which spells out the implications of life lived in the risen Lord and his Spirit; and the Book of Revelation (cycle C), the only piece of apocalyptic literature in the New Testament, which discloses the paschal liturgy of the end times. Of all times of the year the Alleluia or Gospel acclamation should be sung in as festive a fashion as possible and celebrated in a way which leads directly into the proclamation of the Gospel. The sung Alleluia may also be repeated *after* the proclamation of the Gospel. On the subject of music, our English hymnody is particularly blessed with resources for the Easter season. The sequences are hymns that developed during the Middle Ages from the final Alleluia. The two obligatory sequences that remain in the lectionary are the *Victimae paschali* for Easter and the *Veni Sancte Spiritus* for Pentecost. Instead of routinely reciting these works of poetry as a kind of fourth reading, we could, in contrast, artistically present them as a response to the second reading through the creative use of dance, media, choral singing, or instrumental accompaniment.

The homilies should draw their inspiration from these scriptural accounts or from the Easter season itself with its strong emphasis of baptism as the gateway sacrament to the Christian life, the gift of the Spirit as the Easter gift of the risen Lord, and Christian mission or outreach which is our vocation through baptism. It might be helpful to recover the mystagogical style of preaching of the early Fathers of the Church. Only after the celebration of the initiation sacraments (baptism, chrismation, and eucharist) did the Fathers expound on the meaning of the rites and their ongoing significance. At a time when we tend to over-explain symbols in an often superficial way, this could be a good opportunity to lead people into the inner mystery of the sacraments as an encounter with the risen Lord which encompasses the whole person.

The profession of faith might be rephrased in the dialogical form of a renewed or baptismal commitment as done at the Easter Vigil and on the following Sunday. Or again the creed could be alternated with the Apostles' Creed, which takes its origins more directly from the baptismal liturgy than does the more theologically couched wording of the Niceno-Constantin-opolitan creed recited every Sunday. A precedent for this option is already found in the Directory for Masses with Children (no. 49) reprinted in the sacramentary. The general intercessions should voice the same concerns as articulated in the readings or the season and be specially prepared for each Sunday so as to be timely and relevant as possible.

Liturgy of the Eucharist

Be sure to take full advantage of the prefaces, the proclamatory section of the eucharistic prayer. There are five prefaces for Easter, two for Ascension, one for Pentecost. The thematic subtitles can help determine the proper selection. Ideally they are sung with the chants found in the sacramentary.

I.   The Paschal Mystery
II. New Life in Christ
III. Christ lives and intercedes for us forever
IV. The Restoration of the Universe through the Paschal Mystery
V.   Christ is Priest and Victim

This might also be an excellent occasion to ask the assembly to stand during the eucharistic prayer, from the introductory dialogue to the concluding Amen of the doxology. In this way the more ancient precedent of standing for prayer during the Easter season can be recovered, as well as a more active posture indicative of the motif of praise and thanksgiving which makes up the central prayer of the Mass.

The double Alleluia which concludes the Easter Vigil and the Easter Sunday eucharist is continued throughout the octave of Easter and could be fittingly sung on all the Sundays of the Easter season.

In addition to these words and actions, attention could be given to the liturgical environment during the Easter season: tasteful Alleluia banners, fresh spring flowers to accompany the usual array of Easter lilies, and the like. The processional cross could be embellished with a swathe of white cloth emblematic of the resurrection, or the Easter candle itself might be carried in procession. And always remember that all the liturgical options and appointment are subservient to the primary symbol of all and the surest sign of the Holy Spirit: the people of God, the Body of Christ, the church assembled for worship.

Practicing Works of Charity

This aspect of outreach might best be developed by working from within the Christian community outward, for charity begins in the home! In addition to being with the family, the domestic church, there are a number of Easter customs that might be cultivated. The Easter egg is a symbol of fertility and life; our ancestors in the faith saw in the chick bursting out of the egg an image of Christ emerging from the rock tomb. We could learn from the Eastern Church how to color and decorate the eggs in a more ornate fashion. The custom of roast lamb for Easter Sunday dinner well recalls the paschal feast we are celebrating, as also do the pastry delights in the form of a lamb. The tradition of new clothes at Easter is a vestige of the baptismal garments the newly initiated wore during the octave of Easter. (Remember *Dominica in albis* or White Sunday?) The Easter parade is reminiscent of an earlier custom of taking a walk in the field to enjoy the freshness of nature which in turn mirrors the new life of the resurrection. Easter lilies, plants, and candles from the Easter Vigil are other ways of expanding upon the meaning of the Easter season.

The editorial summaries from the preferred Easter readings, the Acts of the Apostles (2:42–47; 4:32–35; 5:12–16), describe the close-knit life of the early Christian community which was of one mind and one heart in the Lord. These early assemblies were not exclusively cultic or sacramental, but rather attended to three basic needs of Christian communities of any age: to hear the Gospel preached, mutual support, and cult (prayer and sacrament). If Joseph Gelineau and others are correct in asserting that our Sunday assemblies should not be exclusively cultic, the Easter season would be an excellent opportunity to encourage a greater sharing among parishioners by encouraging fellowship and community after Mass along with simple refreshments as a kind of extended eucharist. After a long cold winter the usually pleasant springtime weather could be a further inducement to provide for this gathering outdoors as the people leave the church building.

For the newly initiated Christians the Easter season of mystagogy is also devoted towards discerning the particular gift and ministry to which they are called in order to build up the Body of Christ as a sign and instrument of the Kingdom of God at work in our world. To be a Christian is not a vocation to be selfishly guarded or coveted, but only finds its true potential when we share ourselves with a sense of mission in life. The Easter season could be a time for all the parishioners to discover a sense of ministerial outreach. The recovery of the church as mission is one of the foremost needs of our day. The challenges are almost overwhelming: nuclear proliferation and a spiraling arms race, global hunger, flagrant violation of human rights, inflation and unemployment in a worsening economic picture, violence and terrorism.

What better time is there than the Easter season to bring to bear the transforming power of the new creation inaugurated by the resurrection of Jesus Christ? As the church prays in the terse words of the opening prayer for the Sixth Sunday of Easter:

> Ever living God
> help us to celebrate our joy
> in the resurrection of the Lord
> and to express in our lives
> the love we celebrate.

Ordinary Time: The Season of the Year

CHAPTER 16

With the celebration of Pentecost Sunday the church concludes the fifty days of Easter. The Easter candle is removed from the sanctuary and returned to its customary place near the baptismal font. The liturgical color of white yields to green. Ordinary Time (*tempus per annun*) of the church year resumes.

If the Advent-Christmas-Epiphany season highlights the manifestations of the Lord and the Lent-Easter season highlights his paschal mystery, Ordinary Time comprises the other thirty-three or thirty-four weeks in the year which celebrate no particular aspect of the mystery of Christ. Recall the earlier awkward division into two periods of varied length: "time after Epiphany" and "time after Pentecost"; those Mass texts for Sundays after Epiphany were not used because of Lent were transferred to the time prior to the last Sunday after Pentecost. The thirty-four weeks of Ordinary Time now constitute a single season. Ordinary Time commences on the Monday after the Sunday following 6 January (Epiphany) and continues until Tuesday before Ash Wednesday inclusive. It begins anew on the Monday after Pentecost and ends before Evening Prayer I of the First Sunday of Advent.

Ordinary Time thus occupies the largest segment of the litur-

181

gical year and should not be regarded as a nonentity. After all, the church year itself is a sacrament of time when we recall the saving events of the past, appropriate them more fully here and now, with a view toward the fullness of our salvation when Christ comes again at the end of time. Indeed, one could refer to Ordinary Time as "Kingdomtide," a third cycle or season which takes up after the feast of the Baptism of the Lord (reckoned as the First Sunday of the Year), whereby Jesus is solemnly inaugurated as Messiah and Christ and embarks on his public ministry, and culminates in the feast of Christ the King (last Sunday in the church year). In the words of Pierre Jounel, these Sundays of the Year

> are Sundays in a pure state. They have no secondary traits but simply embody the very essence of the Christian Sunday or Lord's Day as presented to us in the tradition of the Church. Each of them is an Easter, each a feast.

Sunday

For some time we have been accustomed to speak of Sunday as a little Easter in the liturgical week. Recent scholarship suggests exactly the opposite is the case: Sunday is the original feast day for celebrating the paschal mystery of Christ crucified and risen; Easter is rather a big Sunday in the liturgical year. We might do well to reflect upon the full meaning of Sunday Mass.

To be a Christian means to be a member of the Christian assembly, the church as it is realized in the local community of the parish. Contrary to some notions prevalent today, Christian existence is not a case of rugged individualism. If there is any recurring pattern or trend in salvation history as portrayed by Scripture, it is this: God calls us by our first name, but always saves us as a people, a church. If the Christian assembly is to be more than a collection of isolated individuals, it must gather together to realize its identity, to be the church. And it gathers together to remember Jesus as he asked to be remembered on the night before he died for us, through the Lord's Supper, the memorial sacrifice he has entrusted to his church.

182

The church community assembles on Sunday and not on some other weekday because Sunday is the day Jesus rose from the dead when he "re-institutes" the eucharist through the "breaking of the bread" (Lk 24:13–36). Sunday is the "day of the Lord": the memorial of his resurrection (first day of the week); an anticipation of his future coming (eighth day of the week); and the day when we here and now assemble to be formed more completely into the Body of Christ which is the church. In this sense the Sunday eucharistic celebrations should be perceived and celebrated as pastoral adaptations of the meaning of Sunday Mass. The Constitution on the Sacred Liturgy of Vatican II sketched this masterful portrait of the meaning of Sunday:

> By an apostolic tradition which took its origin from the very day of Christ's resurrection, the Church celebrates the paschal mystery every eighth day; with good reason this, then, bears the name of the Lord's day or the day of the Lord. For on this day Christ's faithful should come together into one place so that, by hearing the word of God and taking part in the Eucharist, they may call to mind the passion, the resurrection, and the glorification of the Lord Jesus, and may thank God who "has begotten us again, through the resurrection of Jesus Christ from the dead, unto a living hope" (1 Pet. 1:3). Hence the Lord's day is the original feast day, and it should be proposed to the piety of the faithful and taught to them in such a way that it may become in fact a day of joy and of freedom from work. Other celebrations, unless they be truly of overriding importance, must not have precedence over this day, which is the foundation and nucleus of the whole liturgical year. (no. 106)

All this should help dispel some of the incomplete meanings of Sunday. The responsibility for participation in the eucharistic assembly runs more deeply than a mere extrinsic juridical obligation so narrowly and individualistically conceived. The Sunday eucharistic assembly appears to be of apostolic origin (Acts 20:7–12; 1 Cor 16:2) and has to do with the very notion of being church in the New Testament: a universal church manifested in the local community and realized in the eucharis-

183

tic assembly. As John Paul II put it in *Dominicae cenae* (1980): "Just as the Church 'makes the Eucharist,' so the Eucharist 'builds up' the Church." On the basis of these remarks one practice sorely in need of review is the scheduling of Sunday Masses for sheer personal convenience. Until the last century most parishes celebrated a single Sunday eucharist at a time when all communicant members could gather together under the same roof. With the growth of cities and larger parishes, the phenomenon of multiple Sunday Masses developed, but always with the goal of bringing together a sizable and representative grouping of the parish community. In one of his last addresses to a liturgical meeting in 1977, Paul VI—the pope under whose name and pontificate the post-Vatican II liturgical changes were promulgated—urged pastors to reassess and consolidate the times of Sunday Mass so as to realize a greater representation of the eucharistic assembly.

Feasts

Ordinary Time also has its special feasts, in particular the Solemnities of the Lord during the season of the year. They are called "movable solemnities" because their times of celebration depend upon the date for Easter. Of more recent vintage, these "idea feasts" celebrate more a particular truth of faith or aspect of salvation than they do a concrete saving event. The Solemnity of the Trinity was introduced into the universal church in 1334. And yet every Sunday is a Trinity Sunday since the mystery of the Triune God is not only a doctrine to be believed, but is the revelation of the very inner life of God in which we are invited to share. The Solemnity of the Body and Blood of Christ (Corpus Christi) has since 1264 been a kind of reprise continuing the meaning of Holy Thursday. As the full title indicates, the feast has as much to do with the eucharistic cup as it does with the eucharistic bread. The Feast of the Sacred Heart, like other feasts, has been historically conditioned by the piety of the age, in this instance the austere and rigoristic tendencies of Jansenism which refused to accept the overwhelming love of Jesus shown forth in the innermost core of his being. There is also the Solemnity of Christ the King. If the Sacred Heart is a primordial symbol for the abiding love of Jesus, the image of Christ the King—introduced only in 1925 but recapturing the meaning of the Ascension—means that Christ is at the center of our lives.

Other important feasts with fixed dates which are celebrated during Ordinary Time are:

Feast of the Presentation of the Lord (2 February):
a feast celebrated with the blessing and procession with candles
Solemnity of the Birth of John the Baptist (24 June)
Solemnity of Peter and Paul (29 June):
a Roman feast when Eucharistic Prayer I with its catalog of saints would be appropriate
Feast of the Transfiguration of the Lord (6 August):
also the anniversary of the death of Paul VI
Assumption of the Blessed Virgin Mary (15 August):
a highlight of the summer season
Feast of the Triumph of the Cross (11 September)
All Saints (1 November)
All Souls (2 November)
Feast of the Dedication of Saint John Lateran (9 November):
a feast which honors the cathedral of the bishop of Rome

All Saints and All Souls remind us of the life to come—an excellent time to urge people to visit the cemetery—and occur appropriately at the time when Ordinary Time or the season of the year is verging toward its conclusion during the week of Christ the King with the expectation of the second coming of the Lord. "Especially on the last Sundays the mystery of Christ in all its fullness is celebrated."[1]

1. Revised Calendar, no. 43.

185

The Lectionary

The revised calendar is a primary liturgical resource for Ordinary Time, but also are the lectionary and the sacramentary. The Sunday readings from the lectionary are arranged with two principles in mind: a semi-continuous proclamation of the second reading (the Apostle) and of the Gospel of the given Sunday. Moreover, the Sunday lectionary is on a three year cycle: cycle A is given over to Matthew's Gospel; cycle B to Mark; cycle C to Luke. The Fourth Gospel of John is apportioned to the season of Lent-Easter each year as well to the B or Markan year when this shortest of the Gospels is supplemented by reading from John 6, the discourse on the "Bread of Life," during Sundays 17 through 21. This might occasion a series of homilies on the eucharist as the sacrament of the unity of the church. The B year of the lectionary also proclaims as its second reading the following passages from the epistles: 1 Corinthians 6–11 (Sundays 2–6); 2 Corinthians (Sundays 7–14); Ephesians (Sundays 15–21); James (Sundays 22–26); and Hebrews 2–10 (Sundays 27–33).

The Sacramentary

The sacramentary provides a format of presidential prayers for each of the Sundays of Ordinary Time: opening prayer (two options), prayer over the gifts, prayer after communion. These may also be used at weekday Masses when no feast day occurs, although one might also look for suitable orations from the section of the sacramentary entitled "Masses and Prayers for Various Needs and Occasions." There are four eucharistic prayers in the sacramentary to choose from, as well as the appendix with Eucharistic Prayers for Masses with Children and for Masses of Reconciliation which contains three for children and two for reconciliation. A fine catechesis on the much neglected eucharistic prayer could be developed by expounding on the eight Sunday Prefaces in Ordinary Time which each emphasize a different facet of the mystery of Christ.

186

I.   The Paschal Mystery and the people of God (no. 29)
II. The mystery of salvation (no. 30)
III. The salvation of humankind by a man (no. 31)
IV. The history of salvation (no. 32)
V.   Creation (no. 33)
VI. The pledge of an eternal Easter (no. 34)
VII. Salvation through the obedience of Christ (no. 35)
VIII. The church united in the mystery of the Trinity (no. 36)

The prefaces for weekdays could also be drawn upon in this way.

The People

Let us not neglect the most important liturgical resource of all, the people of God assembled for worship. Much of Ordinary Time stretches through the summer months when life is lived at a less frenetic pace and people are more disposed toward taking time for one another. Joseph Gelineau has suggested that our Sunday assemblies include not only ritual celebrations but also opportunities for faith sharing and mutual support. Modest attempts to encourage this fuller sense of the meaning of Sunday would be to provide gathering spaces outside the church where during the warm weather people would feel free to mingle before Mass, or to invite the congregation to get to know one another afterward through the sharing of light refreshments or maybe a picnic after the last Mass as a kind of prolongation of eucharistic communion.

Sunday was originally a day of worship for Christians before it became a day of rest. As a matter of fact, they are days of "sabbath rest" in order to be more completely days of worship. The Sundays of the Year thus provide an opportunity to step aside from our busy workaday worlds so as to allow ourselves to be immersed in the mystery of God and to become more present to one another as brothers and sisters in the Lord.